To Hold The Sun

Handstands and Happiness
on Roatan

Chas Watkins

TO HOLD THE SUN

Find out more about the author and upcoming books online at facebook.com/ToHoldTheSun

Cover and internal photographs © Shawn Jackson, shawnjacksonphotography.com

Cover and book design: by Chas Watkins

Contents

Do what thy manhood bids thee do
from none but self expect applause;
He noblest lives and noblest dies
who makes and keeps his self-made laws

The Kasidah of Haji Abdu El-Yezdi
Richard Burton 1880

An Assignment

"I'm not very original," Paul explained. "Everything we have discussed has been known for hundreds, maybe thousands of years. It's just that now we have the science to understand it all."

"Then why is it not taught more? Why aren't people using the tools you have shown me?"

He just smiled and shrugged.

"They could help a lot of people," I added.

"You tell them then," he suggested, a hint of seriousness slipping into his voice. I looked into his eyes and knew he meant it.

"Maybe I will," I thought.

My editor waved me into his office. He was a smallish, compact man with an implacable manner, so driven he hardly left the office during the day. Waving me to the chair opposite him, he hung up his phone and wrote some notes in a small pad on his desk. He sat back in his chair and looked me over.

"How's it going?" he asked.

We both knew I had hardly worked in months and was barely scraping by. *"I hope I'm not going to be fired,"* I thought. I needed this job. The work I was being commissioned for hardly paid the bills, but it paid some of them. No one needed investigative reporters anymore.

"Really good," I said. "Lots on my plate."

He nodded slowly in agreement, with a look of disbelief clearly on his face.

"Good. That's good," he said. "I have an assignment for you if you can free up the time. Interview and follow up pieces. It requires travel, the subject can only spare a few hours a day so it will take you a week to do an in-depth article."

I practically started salivating - I was going from no work to a cushy travel job with possible additional work to follow. I would be able pay my rent, maybe even pay back some friends.

"I think I can move a few things around, I said trying to keep my tone casual. "Who's the subject?"

"'His name is Paul Haletine. Very strange guy I met at that last conference. No one had seen him before, but he did a few talks and got rave reviews," he said.

"Why is he so strange?" I asked.

"He does handstands," said my editor, raising one eyebrow. "Lots of them. I asked a friend to put me in touch with him. He's an intensely private man, but my friend called in some favors and he agreed to talk about his work."

My editor was always trying to improve himself. He would attend self-help conferences with all the latest ideas on how to fix and improve your life. This I didn't mind, as it got him out of the office and out of our hair. The trouble was, he would bring ideas back with him and test them on us. I had a sudden image of the whole office being coerced into doing handstands. The comical image was not flattering for most of us.

"Unfortunately," he added, interrupting my stream of thought, "this is a personal project of mine. There is no official budget, so I can only scrape together enough to cover your flight and an all-inclusive hotel. There will be no perks and no pay on the first piece either, though it better be good so I can justify paying you for any follow-up pieces."

He stared at me across the desk, a slight smile playing across his mouth.

I was utterly taken aback. Why on earth would I accept such a deal? I had bills to pay. A week away sounded good, but it would be a week when I wasn't earning money.

"I don't think that sounds good. I'll give it a miss if you don't mind," I said, a little peevishly.

He leaned forward across his desk staring at me with a predatory look on his face.

"He lives on the island of Roatan," he half whispered.

My stomach clenched in excitement. Damn it! I was going, and he knew it.

He leaned back in his chair and said smugly, "I took the liberty of arranging your tickets." He picked up a thickly stuffed envelope off his desk and tossed it in front of me.

"The details are in there; you'll leave tomorrow."

Roatan is a long, narrow island off the north coast of mainland Honduras. The largest of the Bay Islands; it is about 47 miles long and 5 miles wide. It's remarkably underdeveloped compared to other nearby islands in the Caribbean, such as the Cayman Islands. Now a territory of Honduras; it has a varied and rich history of pirates and colonial British rule. The island is covered with beautiful beaches, lush jungle, and developments eager to take financial advantage of its unspoiled landscape. A large barrier reef runs along its length, and the reef was the reason my editor knew I could not turn him down.

Ever since I had been exposed to SCUBA diving, I had pursued it with a passion that was only limited by my meager earnings. One of the symptoms of this affliction was having photos of underwater marine life constantly streaming across my computer screen. There were many taken from famous dive sites around the world, but the Bay Islands were prominent in my collection.

I had long nursed the dream of traveling to Roatan, a mecca for the international community of divers. Warm tropical waters and diverse reef life made for some stunning diving. I could not pass up a chance to take up my sadly neglected hobby, especially under the guise of doing actual work.

My flight was booked via Houston. I managed to grab a few minutes in the airport bookshop to pick up something for the two hour flight to Roatan. The tiny bookshop was filled with the latest bestsellers and ever present self-help books. I browsed the self-help section taking in the titles: '*8 Minute Abs*', '*One Hour a Day to Riches*', '*Relationship Recipes,*' '*The 10 Minute Path to Spiritual Enlightenment.*' I calculated that with a two hour flight plus landing and takeoff time, I would arrive on Roatan a married millionaire with the body of a Greek god and the spirituality of the Dalai Lama. I grimaced. The sad thing was that I had already read most of them. Yet there I was - steadily single, unable to pay my bills, tired at the very thought of exercising my body, and uncertain about my direction in life.

I shifted my body to let someone pass between the narrow shelves of books, and tried to look as if I was searching for something more intellectual. I grabbed '*The 10 Minute Path to Spiritual Enlightenment*' and headed to the cashier with a twinge of self-loathing at my selection. I doubted that the changes I was looking for in my life would be solved by the time we landed.

The flight was uneventful and the book, as usual, a disappointment. The highlight of the trip was the descent to Roatan. I could see the green canopy of the jungle outlined by translucent shallow waters seemingly held in by the reef. The reef was a mere few hundred yards from shore. It was marked by small white breakers and the darker indigo beyond which signaled the sudden drop off to deep waters. By early afternoon, I had checked into the Henry Morgan Hotel which was located on the western end of the island; its name yet another reminder of the islands' turbulent pirate history. The hotel opened onto a half mile of pure white sand and leaning palm trees. Known locally as West Bay Beach, it had recently been voted one of the most beautiful stretches of beach in the world. Unlike some of its more famous counterparts it was relatively quiet all year round.

As soon as I had unpacked and settled in I called Paul on my cell. A friendly voice answered the phone. He informed me that later that afternoon he planned to be nearby at a bar called Beachers to enjoy the afternoon. We arranged to meet a short while before sunset for a casual drink so we could introduce ourselves and set up an interview schedule.

I passed the time by walking around and checking out the hotels, dive shops, restaurants, and bars that edged the shore. I easily found Beachers, as it was located very close to the Henry Morgan. The sand in front of the bar was filled with beach chairs. At least half of the chairs were occupied by sunbathers attempting to catch the last rays of the day. The bar, which was made entirely out of wood, was set a few feet above the ground and accessible by steps on either side. Only the left side of the bar and half of the twenty or so small tables were covered by a roof, the rest were exposed to the sun. All the tables had a good view of the beach.

A few families were eating at the tables, their towels and beach bags hung over the backs of the chairs. Little children ran around, barely being kept in check by the adults, grabbing food off the plates and ducking swiftly out of reach. I easily spotted a man sitting alone at the table closest to the beach. He turned as I climbed the steps, and as I tentatively approached him he rose to meet me. He was a tall, lean man of about fifty years old. Muscular and well-formed like a gymnast; he looked and moved like an athlete. He had a shaved head, green eyes, and a tanned narrow face. The crow's feet around his eyes crinkled warmly as he offered his hand and gave me a firm handshake.

"Welcome to Roatan, I hope your flight was good," he said.

"Very quick - I'm surprised how fast I arrived."

We exchanged pleasantries about the trip for a few minutes. I soon discovered he had only been living on Roatan for five years, in a house in the hills above West Bay beach. Though he had agreed to be interviewed as a favor for a friend, it turned out that he had little clue about the focus of the article. I explained that my editor had seen him at a recent conference, and I had been commissioned to put together a series of articles about his work and his life.

"I'm happy to talk about my work at least. The conference was fun, but I only had an hour to talk, so there was much more I would have liked to say," he admitted.

"Well, my editor wasn't able to give me many details about your background, and I could find nothing about you through my research. So maybe you could start by summing up what it is you actually do?"

"Not much!" he shrugged amiably. "I'm semi-retired, so I spend a lot of time with my friends and enjoying the life here. I prefer to keep to myself these days, but I was invited to speak at that conference by a friend. I've always been interested in how we all change and grow, and I have a keen interest in the underlying neuroscience behind those changes. So sometimes I mentor people. People who want to make changes in their lives."

"What kind of changes?" I asked.

He paused for a moment, considering what to say, and then listed off some items. "Help them help themselves, get through painful experiences, kick unhealthy habits, reach goals, but mostly to feel more content and happy in their daily life. There's no magic to how I help; there are no secrets involved. There are many other sources where one can find similar information, though I must admit it's hard these days to differentiate pseudoscience from real science. Everything I do is backed up in some degree by solid research. I'm a skeptic at heart - I don't teach people that they can solve their problems with positive thinking or by asking the universe for gifts. Much of what I do has been practiced for a long time, but has only recently been verified by science. What I can do is demonstrate mental tools which can be used to create change. More than that, I can help you understand yourself a little better, and that knowledge can help you make the changes you desire."

I had read or heard similar claims on the cover of many self-help books. Refreshingly, I did hear a degree of cynicism to some of the dubious commercial methods on the market.

"I'm here for a week, Paul, and I hope to dive every day that I can."

"Evenings will be fine. I need to do some work during the day. I would prefer to meet early in the morning or in the evening. Let's start tomorrow; early, before you set up your diving itinerary. I have an hour free after I exercise. Meet me at the Infinity dock at the end of the beach at 6:30 AM and we can plan out the week. You should be able to find it easily enough, it's at the western end of the beach."

I nodded in agreement.

"Now, since I don't believe you know anyone on the island," he continued, "and I'm joining some friends for drinks tonight, I think you should join us for some food, drink and good company. If that is good for you?"

"Sounds great!" I said. I hadn't been looking forward to spending my first night alone in my hotel room. And it turned out that he was right about the good company; my first evening on Roatan would have been perfect apart from one painful blunder.

It didn't take us long to walk up from the beach to his friend's house. Though the hill leading up to it was very steep, I didn't complain, but towards the end my breathing started to become labored. He hardly seemed to notice the incline, keeping a steady discourse on the island, its inhabitants, and his life since he moved here. I got the feeling that he carried on a one-sided conversation to spare me the embarrassment of talking while trying to catch my breath.

We reached the house as the sun was nearing sunset. It was situated overlooking West Bay, and from this far up the views of the beach and the bay were quite stunning. The majority of the houses I had seen so far were made from wood, and this house was no different; painted a pale blue color that seemed to make it leap out of the surrounding greenery. It was modest in size, but had a large outdoor deck projecting from it which faced out to the bay. I guessed the deck was engineered to exploit the great views that the location provided, and I could hear the rumble of many voices on the deck from our position below.

"That was quite a walk," I said as we climbed up the final steps and knocked on large double doors at the side of the house.

"You should try running it," he said, sighing. "It almost kills me."

As no one answered, Paul let himself in and we made our way up another set of stairs. At the top we entered a large room that combined a modern kitchen and a spacious living area. It was filled with people. Glass doors on one side opened onto to a large deck. Small groups were chatting on the deck as a man walked between them, offering plates of food. At a glance they looked like a decidedly diverse group of people. Some were dressed in suit and ties and others looked like they had just wandered off the beach. I heard a mixture of languages coming from the crowd.

A small, tanned man dressed immaculately in a crisp white suit broke off from one group and made straight for Paul. He thrust out his hand and then pulled Paul into an embrace.

"Glad you could make it," said the man happily, "and you brought us someone new?"

Paul politely introduced me as a visiting reporter and an avid diver.

"Welcome to my home. My name is Piero, and any friend of Paul's is welcome in my house," he said, and then made his excuses and moved off to join his other guests.

"What does Piero do on the island?" I asked, trying to match the Spanish way of rolling the Rs so I would say his name correctly.

With an arch of his eyebrows at my pronunciation, Paul explained that Piero was a very successful lawyer who worked primarily in Tegucigalpa, the capital of Honduras. He then guided me over to a small group of people and introduced me. Listening in to the conversation, I realized that my earlier thoughts had been correct. The room was filled with people from all over the world, as well as a number of locals. In no time at all I was lost in conversation with Paul's friends.

The evening was thoroughly enjoyable; the company great and the food excellent. We were served a mixture of local fish dishes, international appetizers, and wine that flowed a little too freely. The sunset was spectacular from our view over the bay. We could watch as the bright yellow sun slowly descended below the horizon far out to sea. The color of the sky started off powder blue, but quickly transformed from orange to a deep rich red; finally culminating in a dark night sky filled with thousands of stars. When viewed from an island far from cities of man-made light, the stars are so numerous and bright it's awe-inspiring. All in all it was a wonderful and entertaining first night on Roatan. That is, until we made our goodbyes.

As the evening wore on people slowly left, until there was only a small group of us remaining. There was an active social life on the island I was told, and many had moved onto other gatherings. Paul told me he would walk me back to my hotel to ensure I didn't get lost in the dark. As we made to leave we joined our host Piero who was talking to a lovely Honduran lady from the mainland. She spoke perfect English, and we had talked at length earlier in the evening. I thanked him profusely for allowing me to join his party. As I spoke Piero's name, the woman stifled a laugh and looked back and forth between Paul and Piero.

"Come on guys, you have to tell him," she said. "It's not fair to keep letting him do it."

I gave Paul a quizzical look. Piero looked away with a huge grin on his face. He looked as if he was trying to keep himself from laughing.

"What? Tell me!" I said, puzzled.

"Well" Paul started hesitantly and a little awkwardly. "Our host's name is Piero, pronounced 'pee-aih-roh', but you've been mangling it all evening. You've been saying 'pay-rrrho', which is *perro*, the Spanish word for dog. We didn't have the heart to tell you since you were trying so hard to pronounce it, then it just became too funny to raise the subject again."

They burst into laughter and I was glad the color of my face was hidden by the dark.

Flying over West Bay Beach on arrival

2

The Dock

By 6 AM, the beach was already bright with light and the air warm. The tranquil turquoise water barely moved where it met the sand. As I walked along the shore, I felt my face flush slightly with embarrassment. I made a fool of myself during our first meeting, and I was a little worried about the impression I made on Paul. I shook my head, trying to rid myself of the petty anxiety. There had been no maliciousness from anyone, just harmless fun. The host reassured me that he took no offense from my mistake, but, as with all troubling thoughts, I would push it out of my mind only to feel its quick, unwelcome return. The dock where we had arranged to meet was a long, low wooden platform shaped like the letter L, pushing out from the beach in front of the Infinity Bay Hotel. The wood planks were gray and worn, with small gaps in between allowing you to see through to the water below. The walkway was only a few feet off the surface of the water, and was supported by wooden pilings placed every few feet along the outside. I could see a variety of multi-colored fish darting around the pilings, using the shade to hide from the bigger fish.

A few water taxis were tied up to the pilings, ready to pick up passengers and ferry them back and forth from the beach to the restaurants and nightlife of West End, a 10 minute ride away.

I deliberately arrived 15 minutes early for the meeting, as I knew Paul would be finishing his early morning run soon. The night before I had learned of the bizarre ending to his exercise routine from his friends. I wanted to see it up close, so I took a vantage point about 60 feet from the dock and sat on a large rock. Far enough away, in my opinion, to not disturb his routine, but close enough that I could be sure he would notice me. I wanted to be open about watching him.

As I waited, my mind returned yet again to the embarrassment of the previous night. It was such a minor event, yet I had obsessed about it most of the night. Their laughter seemed good natured, but it made no difference. By the time I saw Paul running up the beach towards me I had replayed the event in my mind several times, and each time my body responded with a flush of embarrassment.

Paul ended his run where the dock met the beach and collected his breath. He ran every day and called it his healthiest addiction. He rested for a moment, then turned and started moving towards the end of the dock. Glancing back at the beach, he noticed me sitting on the rock. Changing direction, he began to walk towards me. I waved him back and gestured towards the end of the dock. He stopped, paused, chuckled to himself, and shook his head as if to say, 'Oh, another one has come to watch the show.'

Three evenly-spaced pilings stood at the end of the dock, each about eight inches in diameter. They were made of wood, roughly circular, and cut flat on top. Each one jutted above the dock a few inches, but the middle one was taller than the others by nearly a foot.

Paul took a position a few inches in front of the tallest piling, with his feet together and toes pointing to it. He faced toward the sea; arms by his side, his eyes closed as he took several slow, deep breaths. Then he opened his eyes and slowly leaned forward so that his hands grasped the piling. He rested his palms solidly on the top of it, his fingers tightened onto the sides. Then he tipped himself forward, and with a little bunny hop, brought his knees up to rest on the outside of his elbows so that he was supporting his full weight on his two hands. He held the position, looking much like a frog frozen in time while jumping off a lily pad. Then, in one smooth motion, he tilted forward and pushed his legs up above his body into a handstand.

His body now looked like an extension of the piling; perfectly aligned, with his toes pointing at the sky. Moving slowly, he bent his arms at the elbows. His body gradually descended so the top of his head touched the piling. Then, reversing the motion, he slowly pushed himself back up into the handstand and locked his elbows.

I had seen gymnasts do handstands push-ups in college, but I found it remarkable that a man could do them at Paul's age. I understood from chatting with his friends the night before that doing handstands on the dock was only a recent addition to his exercise routine.

Paul executed eight push-ups flawlessly, each one an identical copy of the one before it. But on the ninth he seemed to struggle; I could see his arms shaking as he pushed himself into the upright position. Halting for only a second, he slowly began to lower his body back towards the top of the piling. Halfway down, he suddenly lost control and, in an attempt to stop his head crashing into the top of the piling, he pitched his whole body onto the dock and collapsed in a heap.

Leaping off my rock, I moved quickly to join him. He was still sitting on the wooden planks at the end of the dock ruefully shaking out his hands when I arrived. Chagrined, he looked up at me.

"Amazing, truly amazing," I exclaimed.

"Which bit? You mean the crash onto the floor?" he said, "Hardly a good ending, it would have been better to land in the sea."

"Why do you push yourself so hard?"

"Normally I don't. I usually do only a few repetitions and do them several times in a day rather than so many at once. Easier to recover that way, and I think repetition is the real key to growth. But when you have an audience there's always a temptation to show off."

He looked at me, slightly embarrassed. "And then I got

my reward," he added, indicating his position on the ground. He pulled himself together and stood up. "How much time do you have before your first dive?" he asked.

"Actually I'm not starting until this afternoon, so I'm totally free."

"Then let's go to the coffee shop for a chat," he suggested.

"Sure. Sounds great,"

As we moved off the dock, he asked what I would like to talk about today.

"You decide."

"Let's discuss and plan our week over coffee."

The JavaVine coffee shop and wine bar was only a short walk from the beach. It was a cozy place, with a wonderful coffee aroma that enveloped you as you opened the door. The walls were painted a warm purple and there were clusters of wooden tables and comfy leather chairs that gave it a very welcoming feel. After stopping to order our drinks, Paul led the way through the other customers to an area that was separated from the rest and dropped into one of two large leather chairs facing a small table. I took the other chair, which was spacious and comfortable. Moments later our drinks were brought to the table.

Cupping his coffee in his hands, Paul casually asked if I had fun the night before at the dinner party. I answered "Yes" a little too fast, and immediately felt my face flush with embarrassment.

Paul looked at me and noticed the flush of my face. "Are you still upset about last night's incident? It really was nothing, we were only having a little fun," he offered apologetically.

"I hardly think calling your host a dog all evening is nothing," I replied, a little indignantly.

Paul stared at me for a minute. I could not read his face. "We thought it was funny, but you're right, we let it go too far."

I sank further into my chair, now writhing in embarrassment.

After a few seconds, he added, "I apologize, you were my guest and I should have taken better care of you. Let me repay you by fixing your discomfort. Fixing small issues like this is as good a place to start. I will show you how to manage pain."

"Pain?" I echoed inquisitively.

"Yes, pain. Well, it would be more accurate to say minor emotional pain. Which you are experiencing right now and I, to a lesser degree, experienced on the dock this morning."

"Though," he said while rubbing his wrists, "there was a good degree more physical pain involved in my incident." He re-settled himself in his chair.

Taking out a small, silver voice recorder from my pocket, I asked, "Do you mind if I record what you are saying so I don't leave anything out?"

"No, not at all, it's easier that way for me as well."

I started the recorder and placed it on the table between us.

"Okay then," he started. "Yesterday I promised you real tools that you can use in your life. Not just words or philosophy, but actual methods to help you. So, by the end of our conversation today you will no longer feel embarrassed about last night. I guarantee it."

Short of a large blow to the head and resulting brain damage I couldn't see how that was possible, but I nodded slowly and tried to keep the disbelief off my face. "That seems fair," I said.

He leaned back in his chair while still looking at me, seeming to search my face for some answer. "Good. You don't believe me. Proof should be necessary for such claims."

'*So much for hiding my feelings!*' I thought.

"First, I think it's important to understand our emotions, especially their purpose," said Paul. "We are the result of millions of years of evolution, and nature is highly efficient and purpose-ful. She wastes nothing, and strives for efficiency in all matters. So there's always a reason behind what she produces. Physical pain is obvious," he said, indicating his wrists, "both in how it works and in its effects. It's a warning of imminent danger or continuing damage to our physical self. The pain response system is one of incredible speed. It can be a little overzealous sometimes, but it's better to overreact to a threat than to be too slow to react."

"If we touch something hot, we are pulling our hand back before we're even consciously aware of the heat. The response is built into our brains, hardwired. We don't have to consider our options. We don't have to ask ourselves if it's really hot. We don't find ourselves saying, '*Hmmm... maybe I should wait for the smell of burning flesh.*' Of course not! Instead, we jump away from the threat," - he jerked his hand back suddenly as if from an imaginary fire and then looked at his hand - "and only then attempt to figure out what happened."

"Emotion is similar in that it's there to help us, guide us and warn us. When the mind is in an intense emotional state, the brain releases chemicals that make that particular experience stick in our memories. That's why we are more likely to remember and learn from any important event."

He paused. Pointing to his temple, he said, "I sometimes use the words brain and mind interchangeably when I do my talks. I usually refer to the brain when I'm talking about physiology or chemistry of the body and the mind when I'm talking about our perception or psychology. But forgive me if I interchange them sometimes.'

"Fear warns us of possible danger. We burn ourselves, and the next time we get close to fire we experience fear. When attacked, we learn to fear the attacker, but we also create a different emotion: anger. We create a state of being which helps us fight back against a threat. Our emotions can also be subtle or strong; one of their primary roles is to help us integrate ourselves tightly into a social group for our protection. We just have to remember that all emotions have a purpose. Even the painful ones."

"Where would embarrassment fit into that viewpoint?" I interjected.

Paul paused for a moment seemingly lost in thought. "I can't give you a black and white answer to that question. I can't say one emotion is there to support this particular process or even 'this is what nature intended it for'. That would be conjecture on my part. Scientific knowledge has advanced tremendously in the last few years with the emergence of new brain monitoring technology. Technology that allows parts of the brain to be observed down to individual brain cells or neurons. Literally, to be able to see what our brain is doing while we think and feel. Each emotion may have multiple purposes and those emotions all have a physiological effect on the body. Anger releases epinephrine, norepinephrine and possibly other chemicals that we are not aware of now."

My puzzled look stopped him. "I don't know what those are," I said.

"Sorry," he apologized, "The exact biological processes are not relevant to our discussion."

"You mean the way adrenaline is released by fear or anger so that you are prepared to fight or run from danger," I suggested.

"Exactly," he said. "To answer your question about embarrassment, I would expect it's there to let you know you did something that lessened your status in your tribe or social group. It's an extremely powerful emotion and is effective in curbing people's behaviors. It works well at maintaining cohesion in a group, which was essential for survival."

"And you are going to strip me of this emotion?" I asked.

"No, not the emotion itself. Just the memory of the emotion you have attached to the specific incident last night," he replied.

"Right," I said, trying to keep my face straight.

He smiled again at the disbelief in my voice. '*I seriously should control that*,' I thought.

"Let me finish my explanation, then I will show you. A demonstration is better than words."

I indicated he should continue.

"Understand that emotions, especially painful ones like fear, anger, loss, jealousy, and humiliation," he paused slightly, emphasizing the word *humiliation*, "have a reason to exist. We must be careful to understand the message they are trying to communicate and understand the ramifications of removing them. For instance, what do you think was the meaning that could be taken from your current—how should we say...?"

I had the distinct impression he was now teasing me. "I would say it would teach me to listen carefully to my hosts name and make sure I pronounce it properly."

"Very good. I think that is an appropriate message, and honestly all there is to be had from this particular incident," he said.

"And that you and your friends have a bit of a cruel edge to your sense of humor," I added.

He tipped his head to me in apology. "You are right there, my friend," he said. "Please accept my apologies once again. Joking is just a sign that my friends like and accept you."

Somewhat mollified, I waved him on.

"So, it's necessary to find the message in the emotion of any particular event. It's not always as straightforward as in your case. Fear and anger tend to be the simplest; but loss, jealousy, envy - all of these can have a subtle message. The meanings may not even be immediately available to you in your conscious mind, but you should try to figure them out before you use the tools I employ. And be wary; you must be honest and not rationalize the message," he warned.

"What do you mean by honest?"

"Well, if you had a nasty fight with someone it would be a natural tendency, though simplistic, to place the majority of the blame on the other person. However, after calm reflection you may realize that there were behaviors that you both exhibited which led to the fight. More importantly, there were behaviors that you failed to undertake to stop the fight in a loving way. I think that if we desire to be truly happy, we need to accept our own mistakes, so we can prevent them from repeating. You can't change another's behavior, but you can and should master your own. Finding the most useful message can take a lot of honesty and self knowledge."

"I can see that it would be difficult to acknowledge our own flaws."

"Yes. And lastly, we have to check if we are trying to rid ourselves of pain that is beneficial to us. For this very reason, I don't often do what I'm about to show you."

"Okay, now you've lost me," I said a little abruptly. "In what way can the feeling of pain be beneficial to us, especially if it continues to make us feel bad?"

His eyes widened a touch at the tone of response, but he continued calmly. "How many life stories have you heard where someone suffered an experience or a series of experiences where the resulting humiliation, anger, fear, etc. drove them to change themselves or meet some heretofore unimagined goal. You could be removing the emotion that pushes you forward to something better. So you must be careful of unintended consequences in messing with your own emotions."

"Well if you take the message from it, won't that be the same?" I challenged.

"No!" he stated emphatically. "Not at all. We are not motivated by words. We are motivated by emotions. Thoughts and plans may direct you, even inspire you, but emotions drive you. Th-" he stopped mid-thought and said, "But motivation is a topic for another time."

He clapped his hands. "Let's get down to business. There are three tools I use to help with emotional conditioning; one is more of a general tool so I will get to that one later. The first one I'm going to demonstrate is meant for a specific event, such as last night. An event that results in a negative emotion which you keep mentally reliving. In this case, embarrassment." A slight twitch of his mouth and an emphasis on the last word confirmed my belief that he was still amused over the incident.

"Yes," I said. I was beginning to feel a little irritated.

"Okay. Can you think of a song that you can sing in your head? It should be something moronic, funny, foolish, or absurd even. If it makes you want to laugh, all the better. The music I use in my head was from a TV show when I was young. There was a comedian in England called Benny Hill. In his show, he had these scenes where all the people in the show would chase each other round and round being silly. The music kept repeating over and over again. Now, in my head, that music is forever associated with the ridiculous and silly and so it works well for me."

I felt confused. "I'm not sure what you want. I need to think of a ridiculous song that is a soundtrack to a TV show?" I asked.

"Exactly. A TV theme or movie soundtrack maybe, but it must be silly or funny."

I drew a blank. "Sing to myself," I muttered. "Silly," I added.

He waited patiently.

Nothing came to mind.

"I have nothing. You see, I can't sing," I added, "I can never hold a tune in my head. Never mind out loud"

He raised his eyebrows. "Nothing at all? What about an advertising slogan, or a song? Those things stick in your head."

Still blank. I looked around the coffee shop looking for inspiration. My eyes wandered around until they rested on a margarita glass. Then suddenly, there it was in my head. I remembered being in a Mexican restaurant and singing a birthday chant. A sing song chant the staff would shout at the table. It was so simple that even a musically stunted person like myself could remember. I sang it out loud:

Happy happy Birthday, from the Chevy's crew,
We wish it was our birthday, so we could party too. Olé!

"Olé! What was that?" Paul exclaimed, echoing my final cry.

I explained that I grew up with my family in California. It had become a tradition that our parents would take us to a Mexican restaurant chain on our birthdays. We always looked forward to it. The restaurant staff would surround the table and chant that short song to whoever had the birthday. All the regulars in the restaurant joined in with the singing. It was a silly yet fun family ritual.

"Perfect." He rolled his tongue like a Spanish-speaker, so he practically trilled the Rs. "Absolutely perfect! You've hit on the perfect song. I wish I had that one in my head too, but it has to be personal. It has to have emotional content for you," he said, "Okay here we go, close your eyes and follow my instructions.'

"Imagine your experience last night. Imagine it as a movie on your TV or computer. You have control of the remote. See yourself actually sitting in front of the movie. Watch yourself using the remote. You can make the screen go back to the start by pressing a button - fast forward, rewind, loop, all the normal buttons. But this is a magical remote. It can do anything you can imagine. It can make all the people wear silly hats, it can remove their clothes, change their faces to look like little piggies. Anything you can dream of it will do for you." He paused. "Do you understand?"

I still had my eyes shut. "Yes, TV screen. A magic remote. Got it." I was feeling a little self-conscious sitting in a coffee shop with my eyes closed.

"Okay, think about where the action would start and stop when you see it in your head. Make sure you get the whole event in the movie."

"Okay," I said.

"Now play it forward on your TV. But faster than normal so people are moving a little faster and their voices are going all squeaky like the chipmunks." I did, and chuckled.

"Good. The fact that it made you laugh is great. When you get to the end of the movie, run it backwards, starting at the end. Now they are all squeaking, moving fast, and they are going backwards."

I did as he asked; this was getting quite amusing. Seeing them all race around backwards and squeaking kept the smile on my face.

"Okay now run it forward again but now put birthday party hats on everyone and have lots of people on the outside chant your song. Over and over again. At the end everyone stops, jumps, and does a whopping "*Olé!*", and the motion continues. Backwards and forwards."

By now the image in my head was totally absurd. I had Paul and all his friends racing around, squeaking out loud and jumping for their "*Olé!*" every few seconds.

"Now," Paul said, "run the video back and forth a few times doing everything I have said. Take your time, and let me know when you have done it at least 10 times."

I ran it backwards and forwards as instructed. The last time I was becoming bored and finished it at high speed.

"Done," I said firmly.

"Open your eyes and look at me." I blinked at the light a few times as I opened my eyes. I must of had them closed for a good 5 minutes. I looked at Paul.

"How do you feel?" He asked.

"I feel good. That was pretty funny. What next?"

"There is no next. That's it, you're done."

I didn't know what he meant for a minute. I remembered last night just the same. Then suddenly it hit me, I had the same memory of last night, but the embarrassment was gone. There was no emotional reaction. None.

Paul watched my face with interest as the realization spread. "Strange isn't it?" he said.

"What did you do?" I demanded, "I mean the memory is still there, but it does not feel the same. I can't even make myself feel embarrassed about it."

"I didn't do anything," he replied, "you did it. I just showed you how. You can do it with any memory you want. You might have to do it a few times with particularly upsetting memories. The only way it fails is if you don't feel the scene is funny or absurd enough, or you're not recalling the actual event. It needs to evoke emotion in you. Also, for particularly powerful events, I have the person look at themselves looking at themselves watch the movie. The addition of you viewing yourself viewing yourself is peculiar but actually helps distance you from the original emotion."

"So I have kind of canceled a painful emotion out with a good one?" I asked.

"That's one way of thinking about it. Your mind does not actually store a video of events in your head. It reconstructs the memory when it needs it. It flows from one point to another along what I call a memory track, reconstructing it. The greater your emotional state when you encoded it, the stronger the memory will be. In your case, the memory track is strong because you were embarrassed when you encoded it. When you travel along the memory track, you feel the humiliation as the brain reconstructs the event. By going back and forth along the memory track and changing the emotion linked to it, you confused your brain. It can't now recreate the event the way you originally remembered it. Understanding how it works is not necessary. It works."

"Did you invent this yourself?" I asked.

He shook his head. "No. I have been using that particular

technique for almost 30 years. I think it came from a practice called Neurolinguistic programming, which is actually a pseudo-science, but I know from experience this part actually works."

I was kind of surprised that a technique such as that was not well known. I mentioned this to him, and he agreed. We talked a little about how people could benefit from such a technique.

"I want you to understand. When I use analogies like memory tracks, they are just that: analogies. The analogy breaks down if you push it too far. But it's useful to discuss this technique in those terms. There is much we don't know about the nature of memory, but it's undeniable that experiencing strong emotion at the time an event happens ensures the memory is stronger than normal.'

"I have one more technique to show you today," he added, "and this one is far more important and far more beneficial to your life and mental health."

"That's quite a claim after that demonstration."

Paul paused thoughtfully for a moment. "There's a saying in the exercise market. 'No pain, No gain.' I've never been a fan of that phrase. I don't see why you have to hurt your body to grow it. A little discomfort, yes. But hurt, no. This tool can difficult to use at first, especially for the first few tries. But the benefits are enormous. It's just that lots of people don't like to do what I ask."

I was both intrigued and a little concerned. What could it involve, electric shocks? "Why?" was all I said.

Pausing again for a second and playing with his empty coffee cup, Paul began to explain. "I assume you're familiar with visualization, as it's pretty common these days in self-help books and on daytime TV shows."

"You mean where you imagine the goal or object you desire and the universe manifests it for you?" I said.

Paul looked a little disgusted. "No, I'm not a believer in *The Secret,* or that sending out positive vibes into the universe is particularly beneficial to you in a material sense. Call me crazy, but visualizing something outside of yourself doesn't change any aspect of the world. It can and does change your attitude to the world but not the world itself. I'm not a believer in being overly optimistic all the time either."

His lack of optimism was a bit of a surprise to me, and I would steer the conversation back to that later.

"What I want to show you is a visualization technique. If you ever had a doubt about the power of visualization or the existence of the *mind-body connection* then it will be gone after this practice."

"Okay let's do it," I said, eager to try it.

Leaning forward, he asked, "Have you ever had someone hurt you, or do something in such a way that you can't get them out of your head? To the extent that you obsess about them? Either because you fear them, were hurt by them, or maybe you just feel some sense of injustice? You keep visiting events involving them over and over again. The constant revisiting of events is disturbing you, and maybe even ruining the quality of your life. It could be an ex lover, a bully, a family member, a stranger even; anyone who somehow has managed to become a painful obsession." He sat back and patiently waited for my answer.

I thought about it. I knew what he meant, though the way he portrayed it as an obsession seemed a little dramatic. Yes, I remembered times in my past when a breakup or an incident had haunted me for days, sometimes weeks, until I finally let it go. But I had nothing like that going on at the moment.

"Yes," I answered truthfully, "I do. Not right now though. There are times when that has happened to me. I once heard a quote that seemed to fit the situation well: *Being angry with someone is like giving them free rent in your head.*"

Paul's eyes crinkled at the corners. "Yes, quite apt. They don't even have to be around. In fact, they can be entirely gone from your life, but you are constantly revisiting the distressing emotions that you associate with them. Well, this tool will help you reduce their presence and the resulting negative effect the thoughts produce in your life."

"But as I said, I don't have that feeling in my life right now. I'm not upset with anyone, so there is no way we can test it."

"Oh, there are many ways to use this tool. Tell me, do you have someone in your circle of acquaintances that irritates you?

Maybe someone you intensely dislike, but can't get away from. Maybe you work with them or just see them every day."

I mentally searched through my friends, acquaintances and work colleagues. But the answer was obvious from the moment he had started talking. "Yes," I sighed, "my brother in law. The man drives me crazy. He's pompous, arrogant and never shuts up. I honestly have never understood what my sister sees in him."

"Maybe your sister sees an altogether different side of him," he suggested.

"Maybe, but doubtful," I joked.

"Anyway, he sounds like a good prospect for us." said Paul. "But if we do this I want you to try to follow my instructions, and not give up because you don't feel like doing it."

"I will," I promised. I was quite happy about the possibility of visualizing him running backwards and forwards in his underwear as I had done with Paul's friends moments before.

"Now, I want you to relax, sit back in the chair, and close your eyes."

I looked around the cafe. I was glad we were sitting so far from everyone else. "Am I going to use my music again?" I asked.

"No," he said, "relax. I want you to imagine someone you love unconditionally, preferably someone innocent like a child. But it can be a parent, grandparent or sibling. Anyone who you feel that way towards. It can even be an idealized person like an angel or your God if you have one. Just as long as you can actually feel the emotion. Imagine them and see them in front of you. Really try to see them in your mind's eye. Then with them in front of you, just open your heart to them and send them as much unconditional love as you can."

I imagined my sister's son. So tiny, cute and playful. Always mispronouncing my name and hugging my leg. I placed him squarely in front of me. I opened my heart and sent him all my love. It was more difficult than it sounds. You can love someone, but how do you send love to them?

Almost as if he were reading my mind, Paul added, "Many people find it helps to visualize their love as a stream of light and warmth pouring from them into the other person."

In my mind, I made light burst out of my heart. It expanded like a floodlight; the light covered my nephew and poured into every part of him. Now it seemed easier. Easier, but not easy.

"Oh, and it helps if you force a smile while you do this" added Paul.

I pulled my face into a forced grin, as I had promised to follow Paul's instructions. Initially it felt false, but it quickly became more natural. *"It's hard not to smile when you are feeling love like this,"* I thought.

"Do think you have it?" asked Paul.

"Mmhmm," I grunted.

"Okay, try to get a grip on what this feels like to you. How your physical body feels. Is your stomach clenched, are you breathing differently? Get in touch with your body and register how it feels. Is it relaxed? Feel how the light comes from your body; where it comes from, what color it is, how it touches the one you love. How do they look?"

It was difficult to catalog my experience during the exercise, but after a few minutes I felt I had succeeded. My stomach was slightly clenched. My breathing slow. The light was a pink color, and it seemed to me that it was warm. My nephew looked happy.

But then I got this sickening feeling. I knew what was coming next. "No," I said. My eyes flicked open.

"You said you would try!"

Reluctantly, I closed my eyes again and went back to thinking about my nephew. I concentrated on sending him love until I felt relaxed again.

Paul gave me a few minutes to calm down. "Now I want you to put your brother-in-law there instead," said Paul.

My suspicion was right, but I had promised to try it. I replaced my nephew with my brother-in-law. To my surprise; while difficult, it was not impossible. Almost as if the light wanted to slip away from him. And my brother-in-law didn't have the same kind of smile on his face, just his usual arrogant manner.

"Try to make sure you feel the same way, that you are still

trying for unconditional love, you are still smiling, that all the image feels and looks the same. The more problems you have with this person the more difficult it is to do this."

I forced a smile on my face. I tweaked the image, made his smile more natural, and made the light pour into my brother-in-law the same way as it had for my nephew.

He was right, it was difficult, but I was coping. It wasn't nearly as hard as he had made it sound.

"Now, I want you to do exactly as I tell you. We are going to change the image a little, and I want you to keep feeling the same emotion. Try to keep your heart open and the love going no matter what you may feel. Okay?"

I nodded my assent and tried to keep the strong sense of foreboding under control. What did he have in mind?

"I want you to bring your brother-in-law as close as possible to you, so he is in your personal space, and wrap him in your arms. Give him a giant hug and give him all the love you can. Keep the love flowing all the time."

My heart sank. I tried to bring him in close. The closer he was, the stronger my feelings of irritation became, and my heart began to beat faster. I never liked the jerk, and now I was imagining us hugging, bathed in some kind of love light. Argh!

"Keep it up," encouraged Paul, sensing my discomfort. "Try and keep the feeling together."

Holding him there was so hard because I was so uncomfortable with the scene I was imagining. I tried to pour love into him, but I was irritated!

Eventually, Paul called a halt to the exercise and told me I could open my eyes.

"How do you feel?" he asked.

"Irritated!" I spat out. My heart was beating faster and I felt repulsed.

"I totally understand. It's completely normal to have this reaction." Paul explained. "It is often how people react at first. What is difficult is that imagining them physically close magnifies the feelings they evoke."

"What's the point of irritating myself?" I asked.

"Well, think about your brother-in-law. How do you feel about him?"

"The same," I said emphatically.

But then I thought about it a little longer. "I'm not sure," I said. "Something is different, but I can't put a finger on it. He still irritates me though. That hasn't changed."

"This takes time to work. I want you to practice this at least four times before we meet tomorrow. Do it for no more than three to five minutes. Will you commit to that?"

I gulped. "Yes, I can do that." I managed a fake smile that I'm sure looked more like a grimace.

He stood up and gently touched me on the shoulder. "You did well. It's hard, but I promise that I'm not torturing you without a reason. You wanted to know how I work. What better way than to experience it? I will see you tomorrow, then. Shall we say 7 AM at my house?"

"Sounds good."

With a nod, he got up and walked out of the coffee shop. I just sat there waiting for my emotions to settle down. 'This is going to be a difficult few days,' I thought.

View from the dock at Infinity Bay

3

Conditioning

"So how do you feel?"

As he spoke, Paul placed his hands idly on the table and slowly splayed his fingers as if he was about to support a handstand. We were sitting outside on the deck of his house. His small wooden *casa* was perched on the top of the hill behind West Bay Beach, and looking eastward you could see all the way down the island. The jungle canopy stretched out for miles along the center of the island, only interrupted by the occasional building and the faraway town of Coxen Hole. The green of the jungle complemented the light blue of the surrounding sea. It was an amazing view, and it was easy to get lost in thought following the beautiful coastline with your eyes. There was a good breeze, which I was grateful for as otherwise I would've been sweating profusely. Paul was dressed casually as always, shorts and a t-shirt.

"I did my practices as promised," I replied, "and yes, I feel a little differently about my brother in law. I still don't like the guy, but thinking of him doesn't bring up the same intense and instant revulsion as it did before."

"Was it uncomfortable to do?"

"Very!"

"It gets easier with practice, I can assure you, but it's very difficult at first. Thank you for putting in the effort," he said. "Lots of people give up which is terrible because it's so beneficial to them."

He continued, "The idea is not to change or improve your relationship with him really, though it will. The idea is to change your feelings about the person. To remove the negative emotions that actually hold you back. It works in several different ways, and you can rid yourself of the harmful effects of jealousy, anger, irritation and even sadness. The act of sending love rewires the brain, so to speak."

"Have you used it much yourself?" I asked.

"Every day I use it as part of my meditation. When I have no relationship or event that I need to work on today, I might just pick some acquaintance at random, or even a stranger to use in the exercise. To my mind it's no different than a mechanical way to achieve the Buddhist ideal of compassion. Maybe it's identical, I don't know. It's a simple and effective tool for me. A tool to rid you of negative emotions and bring compassion into your life."

"So you find it makes that much of a difference," I said.

"Oh yes. I first discovered it when I was completely obsessing over some injustices that a friend had committed against me. I could not let it go. All day long I would find my mind going back over and over the events. Finally, I thought 'I will be the bigger person. I can't change her, so I will forgive her.' I started sending her thoughts of goodwill, and eventually I modified it to the form of visualization I showed you. Then my obsession stopped."

"And then you were able to forgive her?" I asked.

"No," he laughed, "then I went and apologized to her. You see, I was so wrapped up in the injustices that had been done to me that I failed to see the truth. It was mainly my own actions that had caused my friend to behave the way she had. In actuality, I shouldered the majority of the blame. But I couldn't see that because I was too close to it. So from that point onwards I made visualization part of my daily routine. It has a great ripple effect."

"Ripple effect?" I prompted.

"Yes. When you practice something, good or bad, or make a change in one part of your life, it carries over to other parts of your life. Obviously we only want to make positive changes, but in life we often make unhealthy choices, which can affect all areas of our lives."

Paul paused for a minute. He asked if I would like something to drink. Though it was warm, the full heat of the sun wasn't yet hitting us, and I was loath to interrupt his train of thought.

"No, go on."

"You see real change in your life. Dramatic and permanent change is possible for everyone. It's just most of the time people go about it the hard way and so they usually fail."

"What do they do wrong?" I asked.

"Well first, we want it all and we want it now! It seems to be part of our culture these days. That just does not work. Every now and then something will happen that forces us to take inventory of our lives, often prompted by an external event. A new year starting, or a birthday perhaps. Sometimes it's just an incident of some kind that makes us wake up to our surroundings. We realize we're not happy and we decide to change. But as we know from years of New Year's resolutions, that seldom works. Within a few weeks, sometimes days even, we are back to our normal routine with just regret and a little self-loathing as our reward."

"So what is the easy way?"

"Studies of people who have totally transformed their lives have shown that, in each case, there is usually one habit they manage to change which once changed has caused a ripple effect throughout their lives. Often that change is maintaining an exercise routine.'

"Let me give you an example. You decide to start exercising to help your health. You make a regular time every day to go for a half hour walk. After maintaining the routine for a month or two, you feel fitter. You become interested in nutrition, so you start to watch what you put in your mouth. You lose weight. You feel healthier, and your attitude changes. You feel calmer and more able to cope with issues. You become more productive at work and others notice. You gain respect in their eyes. Your self-esteem grows. You start exercising with friends. Maybe social walks. It becomes a virtuous circle, all brought on by one event. In this particular example you committed to walking 30 minutes a day. You kept to that commitment and made it part of your daily life. The rest just followed along. That starting habit; the pebble in the pond that starts the ripples, could be something like stopping smoking, becoming a vegetarian, or even taking up dance!"

"So you are saying to focus on one goal at a time," I said.

"Yes, exactly!" answered Paul. "Though I don't like the way goals are emphasized so much these days, especially timed ones. A goal implies a stopping point at which point something has been achieved, and you are done. If you don't achieve it by a certain time, you are a failure. I'm more interested in creating a lifestyle change, and then the goals will take care of themselves. Habits are the key to making lifestyle changes. You need to make any new aspect of your life as natural as putting on socks every day."

Paul pulled his foot out from under the table so we could both see it. His feet were bare. "Maybe I need to think of a better example now I live on an island." Putting his foot back under the table, he continued.

"The new habit has to become part of your life. Research shows it takes about 30 days to install a new habit. I think you can also tell when it's integrated into your behavior because you start to crave the new habit when you have to forgo it for some reason. For instance, if I miss my run for a day or two because of the weather I start getting irritated about it. I want to run, or at least walk on the beach! Goals are only beneficial because they are like stepping stones that let you know you are progressing and keep you on the path."

I saw an opening to ask about his habit of doing handstands. "Why do you do handstands, and why so publicly? Are they goals to help you keep to your exercise commitment?"

Paul got up from the table and moved the small distance to the edge of the deck where he leaned against the railing and looked out at the view.

"Yes, and more," he replied after some thought. "To me, handstands are my pebble in the pond. They are the start of my ripple effect. A few years ago I was suffering from depression, and I was meandering down the beach. I had been reading a book about exercise in an attempt to get myself energized. I had read that exercising was as effective as drugs for depression. In the book there were pictures of some people doing handstands. Having never done a headstand in my life, never mind a handstand, I was thinking, '*How cool it would be to be able to do that?*' Then I saw the dock, and somehow combined the two in my mind. I knew what I wanted to achieve. When I look back I can see that as the start, even though it was slow. At first walking, then nutrition, running, strength exercises. All ripples heading outwards but slowly impacting every facet of my life."

"So your dream was to do a handstand on the dock?" I asked.

He turned and said enigmatically, "No. My dream was to hold the sun in my hand."

"What on earth does that mean?"

He sat back down opposite me. "I'm sorry, I can be a little dramatic sometimes. I've never told that to anyone before. I don't believe in telling people my goals or dreams that I have not yet reached. I believe a personal dream shared is a dream diluted."

"I thought you were supposed to tell people your goals in order to enlist their help?" I pointed out.

"No, I don't believe so," he said. "If you need a support group, like when you are quitting an addiction then yes, the support of those around you can be extremely beneficial. But for your own personal goals; no, I don't believe so. I have found there are two different reactions when you open up and tell people your goals. Neither of which help you much. Either they congratulate you on it, at which you feel a small sense of pleasure. Pleasure at being congratulated on something you have not yet done. Now, you're less likely to achieve your goal because your brain has already received a reward just from the congratulatory comments. The other reaction is your friends can show disbelief or discouragement at your goals. Sometimes your friends' perception of you can be a serious hindrance to change. I have transformed the way I look physically through many hours of exercise and a thoughtful approach to nutrition. I avoid eating processed foods and any sugar. Instead of supporting me in my choices, some friends would criticize it. As if I'm being fanatical, and they reasonable. I prefer making healthy choices, so I don't share my goals. Only my achievements."

Pausing Paul took out his phone. "Let me show you something." It was one of those overly-large smart phones that dwarfed mine. He laughed as if he could read my mind. "Yes, it's large." he said, "I like it because I love taking photos, and it's easier to see the results with this phone. Here on Roatan there is so much beauty! There are so many opportunities to take pictures. Look at this one."

He handed me the phone. I saw a photo of someone that looked like him. But whereas now he had the body of a gymnast, in the photo he was at least forty pounds heavier with an extremely large belly.

Frowning, he said. "Yes, I was partial to my beer in those days. Still am sometimes."

"Quite some change," I said. "Especially at your age."

"Yes, that was taken at least three years ago." Taking his phone back, he said, "Let's return to talking about habits in general, as they are important to make any real changes in your life."

"Okay," I said.

I felt he was directing the conversation away from discussion of his personal goals. Judging from his demeanor, I would not get any more information about his future goals for now. "So, if you want to radically change your life you still need to focus on one change at a time." I said summarizing his point. "Understood. But how do you that? How do you find the willpower to carry through on that one change?"

"Willpower," replied Paul. "Reliance on willpower is the second mistake most people make. To explain that, I'm going to have to talk a little about how modern research has shown our brain works. Our brains use a large amount of the energy our body needs daily to survive. The tasks the brain does are amazingly complex. Even seemingly straightforward tasks such as taking a drink. Judging the position of a cup and then moving it to your mouth," Paul mimicked the movement with his hand as he spoke, "is a remarkable accomplishment. Yet we do it unconsciously. We can even do difficult tasks such as driving a car while daydreaming. Part of our brain is always paying attention of course, but after continuous practice some tasks become automatic. They are so ingrained that we can focus our conscious thoughts elsewhere. When a task becomes this automatic we call it a habit and we don't need willpower anymore. It has become part of our lives."

Paul reflected, "I find it astounding that people used to say that we only use ten percent of our brains. As if nature is so extravagant and inefficient that it built in that much extra capacity. Though as always there were plenty of self-help gurus ready to help you tap into these magical reserves for a fee. It would've been less arrogant and more honest to say we haven't figured out how the other ninety percent is actually used. At least we are aware now it's all used, even if we don't understand all its inner workings."

Adjusting himself in his chair, he continued, "So what does all the current research tell us about willpower? Willpower is when we consciously direct our attention somewhere. It's used when we need to suppress a desire or emotion, when we try to control our thoughts or automatic processes. It's exactly what the words *will* and *power* describe: it's when we express our will internally and use our power to control our brain. To force it to do what we want."

"You make it sound as if we are at war with ourselves," I said.

"Yes we are often in conflict. Most of our stress comes from those conflicts. If you want to understand the mind, it's often good to imagine the brain as a distinct set of desires all competing to be heard. I believe that until you can learn to acknowledge those desires, accept them and let them go, it's difficult to reach true peace of mind."

"But back to the point. It turns out that we only have a limited amount of willpower to use at any one time. When that is used up self control becomes very difficult for a while. At least until we can rest. This is technically called *ego depletion*. Everyone has experienced this in one form or another. The mother whose child nags them incessantly until they finally just give into their child's demands, or the shopping trip which lasts too long until you will just buy anything to end it, or the dieter who resists the temptation all day only to indulge at the end of a long work day. All examples of our willpower actually running out after too much control has been exercised."

I nodded my head. I could easily remember one disastrous shopping trip when I was decorating my apartment. I had ended up picking a terrible color paint for my walls. After several hours of looking at color after color, I had became frustrated and tired. I suddenly just picked one on impulse just so I could go home. I still looked at that particular mistake every morning.

"If we depend solely on will power we are doomed to fail," he continued, "and sadly see it as a failure on our part. I hear many people berate themselves with the line, 'I just don't have enough willpower.' They are correct, but this isn't a failure on their part. It's just the way it is for everyone."

"What is the answer, then?" I asked.

"Well the first thing is to eliminate as much as possible the need for willpower. For instance, if you were changing your lifestyle to eat healthy food. Get rid of all the unhealthy food in the house. Never go shopping for food when you are hungry. Keep eating healthy snacks regularly so you don't become hungry near temptation. Or if you are going to start an exercise program, get up earlier. Put your walking shoes and the required clothes by the bed the night before. Make it your goal simply to get out front door dressed to exercise every morning. The exercise will follow once you are through the front door. At every point, you need to figure out what it is that requires you to use willpower, and then as far as possible, eliminate it from the process."

"That makes sense, I guess," I said. "If I don't have temptation in front of me, then I'm less likely to veer from my chosen path. So what else?"

"Then we have to convert our desired behavior into a habit. Once you create a habit, it will actually take willpower to stop the new behavior. We have effectively made a new default behavior for our brain. To convert any behavior into a habit requires understanding how habits form. There are four necessary components that make up a habit in my mind: the trigger, the action, the reward and, of course, repetition.'

"The most important part is repetition. You obviously can't have a habit by doing something once, but how many times or how long do you have to do any behavior to install it as a habit? Most experts think it takes around thirty days. From practice, I agree with that estimate, but I also think you can tell when a habit is properly installed when it takes conscious thought to *not* do it. Then when you try not to do it, your brain actually resists you.'

"The second part is the trigger. A trigger is a signal that lets the brain know we are about to do the same behavior again. To make a good habit, or indeed a set of habits, you need a routine. You need to do the same thing every time in exactly the same way if possible. Like to always go exercise the moment you get out of bed, or always prepare a set of healthy snacks for the day before you leave for work in the morning. Routine is the bedrock of good habits and having a routine creates a good trigger for your habit.'

"The action part of habit creation is obvious. it's the actual behavior you are trying to ingrain into your life. The actual exercise, or the nutritious eating.'

"The final part of creating a good habit is reward. You must give your brain a reward, and the best reward for the brain is emotion. As we saw and talked about yesterday, emotion causes a memory to become very strong. In the same way, emotion causes a habit to become ingrained."

"How on earth do I reward myself with emotion?" I asked, completely puzzled.

"Feel it or fake it. It doesn't matter. The brain has a great deal of trouble telling the real from the imagined. If your chosen action was to be out walking for exercise, then take the time to look around as you walk and experience pleasure at the sights and sounds you see. Rejoice in being outside breathing in the fresh air. Similar to our visualization exercise yesterday, feel it on a physical level. When you finish exercising or whatever your goal was to do, you need to exaggerate how good you feel about completing it. Amplify the sense of joy at completing the task. Reward your brain."

I paused for a moment, collecting my thoughts. "If I can summarize," I said carefully, "first remove anything that may tempt you away from completing an action. Second, repeat the action. Third, make the action identical if possible. Fourth, do the action and while doing it, feel good about it."

"Very nice summary," acknowledged Paul.

"What happens if we don't want to add a new habit. We want to rid ourselves of an old one?" I asked.

"Sadly, you can't. You can't completely unlearn a habit, even if you manage to stop doing it. It's always there in the background. Similar to an old road that is replaced by a newer highway. You may travel the new highway every day, but it's easy to slip back onto the old route if you are not careful. It's why after ten years of not smoking an ex-smoker can be distracted and suddenly find a lit cigarette in their mouth with everyone staring at them. The best thing you can do is substitute another behavior to replace the original one. To do this, you must identify the routine part of the habit, the trigger, and then try to replace the action with a new one and reward yourself. It's not always easy, but you can reform the habit. However, even if you manage to use the old trigger for a new action the old action is still there, waiting in case it's ever needed.'

"As an example, often in my life while working I would go raid the fridge, find a snack, or drink too much coffee. One strategy to fix this was to make sure the snacks were all nutritious, but I couldn't always control my environment. The second strategy was to find the trigger and substitute a replacement action. So first I figured out why I was getting up from my desk in the first place. It usually happened when I got stuck in my work or was over tired I realized I was just trying to clear my head, to find a new approach to my problem. My method to clear my head was to get up and pace around. Often my wanderings would lead me into the kitchen. Once there, my normal eating routines would unconsciously take over. I would put the coffee on, grab a handful of peanuts or an easy snack while my mind was distracted. Then after a short while, I returned to my work. At the end of a long day the peanut can would be empty, and I would be shaking from the caffeine. Not only was I consuming a lot of calories, I was giving myself insomnia."

"So what did you do?" I asked.

"I found a set of exercises I could do when I stood up. I re-arranged my work area so I could either go stare somewhere pretty away from the kitchen, or I could do simple exercises like pull-ups or squats. Then the next time I had to get up to think about something, I went over and did just a few exercises. Nothing too strenuous to make me sweaty. Just enough to get the heart beating a little faster and distract my mind. Then I would return to my seat to continue working. It took awhile to change over. About thirty days," he said with a quick grin, "but now it's automatic and at the end of the day I have used calories exercising, not added them by eating. It also stops me from being too sedentary, which is an issue for all of us that work in front of a computer screen."

Paul raised himself from his seat and stood, "I think we have done enough for now. Unfortunately, I have plans for the rest of today and most of tomorrow, but I have some things that I would like you to think about, and maybe we can discuss them if we go to the fire show tomorrow evening?"

I happily agreed. There were some places I wanted to visit in West End tonight, and I was meeting up with some diving buddies, so his plan worked well for me.

But when Paul told me what he wanted from me, I was left feeling a little disturbed.

Diving with a turtle

4

The Inner Voice

The sun rose too early on Roatan, at least for me that day. I was still tired from the night before, as the parties in West End had gone late into the night, but I had set my alarm early enough, and I was determined to experience the sunrise this morning. I rushed out of bed without showering, as I only had twenty minutes to get to the spot I had picked out to watch it. In the pre-dawn light, navigating my way through the hotels and along the beach was not too difficult. There is a small hill behind the Grand Roatan with a road that leads to the westernmost point of the island. I crested the hill and then walked down the opposite side until I arrived at the iron shore that replaces the beach on parts of Roatan. The iron shore is an area of sharp and crazy-looking hard rock that spikes up out of the ground. Dramatic and dangerous, it guards the south-facing part of the island from the deeper sea.

There was a small wooden platform perched above the jagged rocks that could be reached via a walkway from the road. Feet dangling off the end, I sat facing the east and waited. The sun was still below the horizon, but the light already preceding it was pushing the sky through different shades of red.

While I waited, I thought about the task Paul had set me. In his typical straightforward manner, he had asked me to consider who I thought I was. To try to understand how, why and where my beliefs originated. Even to think about where my personality and spirit might reside in my body.

"Please don't come back with some trite philosophies," he had said, "as often people fall back on generalizations and simplifications when asked hard questions. I actually want you to think about yourself and your place in the world. How do you feel about the essence that is yourself? That bit that carries your individual identity."

I was planning a full day's diving, he knew, and I had mentioned I would not see him until the evening.

"That gives you all day to think about it," he pointed out. "Do you define yourself by your actions, your work, your memories? Do you have a soul?" he listed. He had asked me lots of questions; all designed, I'm sure, to provoke me into thinking about my beliefs. The trouble was, the more I thought about it, the more confused I became.

Suddenly, I realized the sun was starting to rise above the horizon. I put my thoughts aside and just let the experience unfold before my eyes. Too quickly the moment was over, only a memory of colors and a feeling of wonder was left as the sun moved higher. Walking back over the hill, I passed a point where I could see the whole of West Bay beach laid out before me. From the heights, I could see the white sandy beach, the shallow peaceful bay and even the reef just below the surface outlined by tiny white breakers. I stared at the view trying to store it safe somewhere inside me so that I could hold it in my memories with the sunrise.

After a while, I moved back down towards the beach. Walking through the Infinity Bay courtyard, I came out on the sand near the dock Paul used at the end of his run. Paul must have run early as he was already out there sitting on the end of the dock. I moved a little closer so I could see him more clearly. One of the many security guards that edged the beach was watching him as well.

The guard noticed my interest in Paul and moved closer to me.

"He dropin' in the water agin," said the guard motioning to Paul with a strong island drawl to his voice.

"What do you mean?" I asked a little troubled.

"Been lookin him for two years now. He didn't know nothing. Always dropin' in the water. He a crazy man. He was really soft, now he hard, brah. He don't drop no more," he chuckled, "he sah crazy old man."

"But you said he's falling again," I said.

"Yes, brah. He be dropin 'gain. Look he all wet up."

Puzzling out what the guard meant, I looked more carefully at Paul - he was soaked. He looked like he had just climbed out of the water sitting there between the poles, dripping wet

I started moving towards him, the guard touched me on the arm and gently held me back.

"No brah, he don restin'."

I stayed in place held back more by the guard's firm conviction that I would be intruding than by his hand. He had been watching him for 2 years and would know his routines. Paul must be having a bad day, which was strange as I had seen him execute a flawless handstand with strength enough to do push-ups while he held his body upright.

"He don ready," said the guard pointing at Paul.

Sure enough, Paul was slowly rising and moving to stand in front of the piling. He stood before it calmly and looked like he was intensely focused on it.

"Boy be crazy," added the guard.

Paul leaned forward. Hopped on to the piling and smoothly went into a handstand. He held it still for a few seconds. Then slowly his right leg moved away from his left leg and then he gingerly lifted his left hand off the piling. He was holding himself erect with just one hand! Slowly, almost imperceptibly, he extended his free hand out while balancing his body by spreading his legs. He had almost extended his hand fully to the left when he misjudged his balance, and in an instant, he was falling. Somehow he directed his fall forward into the water. He tried to roll into a ball as he fell, but he still hit the water hard on his back.

I moved forward quickly towards the dock. This time the guard didn't interfere. His laughter trailed behind me. By the time I had arrived at the end of the dock, Paul had swum around to a rope and was pulling himself swiftly up on the dock again. He saw me approaching and gave me a little embarrassed look. "Graceful, huh?"

I grinned back. "I've seen worse," I said, and then I laughingly added, "not by much though. Are you okay?"

"Yes. I have gotten pretty good at falling these days," he replied.

"What actually were you trying to do?"

He looked at me thoughtfully. I was expecting him to repeat that he liked to keep his goals to himself. But after a small pause he just said, "Maybe before you leave this week I will be able to show you."

I nodded, understanding that this was all he was going to say.

"How is the homework going?" he asked.

"Difficult, but I will have some answers for you by tonight after diving," I said determinedly.

"Which reminds me, I have to get going, or I will miss the boat." I raced off to my hotel to get ready.

The diving was all I had hoped for on Roatan. The boat took a small group of tourists out just beyond the reef to the end of the island, where we did a drift dive along the edge of the reef wall. The staff who led the dive were pleasant and professional, explaining all I needed to know about the local spots and how to avoid having an impact on the reef.

It's always difficult to explain to those who have never dived the peace and sense of serenity that can be found beneath the noisy world above. With little need to move my limbs except the occasional flick of a fin for steering, the current moved me, as if weightless, along the living outcroppings of coral. The colors of the reef were only eclipsed by those of the many tropical fish that darted in and out of the formations, seeking safety from the larger fish that constantly pursued them. My favorite ones were tiny and electric blue. They would hover around the coral in groups. Dashing *en masse* this way and that in panic at any sudden movement

After my two dives, we headed back to shore in the boat. I was tired and elated. I was also glad that there was still plenty of time in the day to rest up and have some time to organize my thoughts before my meeting with Paul.

That evening, I arrived at the Thirsty Turtle just as it was going dark. The fire show was slated to start in an hour, and Paul had mentioned the day before that it was well worth watching. He was sitting at one of the hexagonal tables with a group of people, engaged in what seemed like a lively discussion. I wandered over, not wanting to intrude, but as soon as Paul saw me, he vigorously waved me closer.

"Come sit with us and meet my friends," he said, making room for me next to him. He quickly went around the table, introducing them. It seemed to be a mixed group of islanders, mainlanders and expatriates. As soon as the introductions were over, they quickly resumed their conversation, which revolved around the difficulties of living on an island like Roatan.

"It seems like paradise to you," said one of his friends to me, "but in reality there is much that has to be given up and more that has to be endured for those that live here. At first it's relaxing, but in truth Roatan is a remote place. It takes a particular type of person who can last here."

The discussion, though pleasant, seemed to be an old and worn subject for them. After a while, Paul pointed to another table that was empty. "Let's go over there where you can see the fire show better." I said that I was happy to stay and watch it from here with his friends, but he shook his head and guided me to the other table, explaining that they had no interest in the show. They had seen it too many times before. One of the drawbacks of living here, he said, was the repetitive nature of the entertainment at the hotels. It was designed for a tourist visiting on a one week vacation and so followed a weekly cycle. Generally every day was a repeat of the same entertainment from the previous week. "When fresh entertainment arrives here, it's devoured by the locals," he said.

Sitting down at our new table, Paul asked simply, "so how did it go?"

I pretended to misinterpret his question and launched into a description of my day's diving. Paul listened attentively, seemingly happy to hear my exuberance. I talked at length about all the beautiful sights I had seen underwater. Eventually, though, I fell silent.

"I'm really glad you are enjoying the diving," said Paul, "it's incredible here. But tell me, have you had time to do some thinking about your beliefs?"

I paused. Of course this wasn't the first time I had thought about my place in the universe. However, I had never actually had to explain it to another person, and I wasn't all that confident that my beliefs were well thought out. When he had first asked me, I felt disturbed because it seemed private to me, but there was something about him that made me want to answer him. I just didn't feel like being lectured on the subject.

"First," I started, "I don't regard myself as a religious person. I don't practice any particular faith. But like most people I believe I'm spiritual. I don't know if I have a soul, a spark of the universe inside of me, or even some connection to the divine. To be honest, I feel that those discussions are personal, impossible to prove, and therefore, a matter of one's own faith."

Paul nodded listening carefully.

"I don't define myself by my work or the things I have collected. Even in my short life, I have seen how easily they can be taken away. I guess I see myself more as a collection of my memories, experiences, values and feelings. I see myself reflected in those people I'm lucky to be close to and love, and those who love me. As I sit here and talk to you, I can't physically locate my essence. I just feel like I'm me."

I sat back, gathered myself together and waited. Paul just said gently, "Thank you for sharing that with me. Though it's a private matter to many, I always like to hear what others believe. I also think it's important to analyze who you are now in order to see clearly who you would like to be in the future."

I was a little taken aback. I had expected a discussion of my beliefs at least. I guess after all the thought I had put into my small speech, I was a little disappointed by his reaction.

"Don't you have any spiritual insights for me?"

Paul looked astonished. "Me? No! I don't have any great insight into the spiritual. In fact, I have great distrust of those that believe or say they do," he finished seriously.

He paused for a bit before saying slowly, "I believe we each find our own path. As long as that path includes love and compassion for others, who am I to say what is good or bad, right or wrong in somebody else's beliefs."

I agreed with his sentiment, though I still felt a little let down by the turn the conversation had taken. I had fully expected a heated debate.

"You are always explaining to me the current research about the mind," I said. "What does that have to say on the subject?"

Paul looked lost in thought for a minute as he considered my question, but after a while he focused on me. "Well it's a bit difficult to research spirituality," he pointed out, "but there is something that I believe is crucial to the discussion and is being debated constantly at the moment. There is an ongoing debate about whether we actually have free will or if we are just slaves to our subconscious. Maybe our sense of self is nothing but an illusion created by the brain."

He had my interest now. I motioned to his drink, inquiring if he would like another.

"Yes thanks," he said.

I waved to one of the passing staff. Motioned to our drinks, and indicated two more. "Go on," I said.

"Free will," said Paul, "is very important to me. It's core to all I believe we are as human beings. It allows us to choose who we wish to become and leave behind our individual origins."

He paused as our drinks were delivered, obviously gathering his thoughts. "Let's think about what is known about the brain. It's made up of parts that have specialized functions. Movement, touch, speech, hearing, spatial awareness, vision, etc. And of course the frontal lobe, which is so much more highly developed in humans than animals. Its apparent purpose is to help us understand the future consequences of our actions and inhibit our behavior as necessary. There is also a good degree of plasticity in the brain, which means it can grow and change over our lifetime. Therefore, we are not limited to what we are now; we can change."

"We also know that the different areas appear to work independently and in some ways competitively. It's not like an army where each part follows orders from a superior. The brain is better compared to a meeting of middle-level managers, where each department head is trying to get their own ideas across, often at cross purposes to the other departments. Eventually the mind acts."

He paused, and looking thoughtful, continued. "But who does the deciding between these managers' ideas, and how does it happen? That is central to understanding who we are. What action is chosen and how."

Wondering the same thing, I asked, "So all this happens automatically and unconsciously?"

"Yes, mostly. I'm sure you have had the experience of driving a car for miles and suddenly realizing you haven't been paying attention to the road. You also can't recall what you did during that period of time. Your attention had wandered, and another part of the brain just kept on driving the car. Making turns, obeying the rules while you thought about something else. The brain can carry on some extremely sophisticated tasks without any conscious direction."

"Yes I have done that. Though it's disconcerting, and I often wonder if I did anything dangerous while I was daydreaming."

"Generally, I would say you have not. If anything out of the ordinary happens, the brain will summon you back quickly. I'm not advocating you daydream while carrying out important and dangerous tasks like driving. You should pay attention. It's just something that can happen when you are carrying out a function that the brain has already mastered and feels comfortable doing.'

"Scientists use the terms *'the narrator'* or *'the interpreter'* in order to discuss the concept of our inner voice: the voice that runs our internal dialog. It seems to give us a feeling of consistency and continuity in our lives. It helps us reason slowly and carefully through situations until we find a solution. However this narrator can sometimes get out of hand, especially when we are unhappy. Then it does more harm than good. It can become repetitive and obsessive about problems that are upsetting us."

He frowned. "Sometimes it can be quite awful to listen to internally, especially when we have been hurt in some way. It can go on and on incessantly, keeping our focus on one particular experience."

"Like this," he tilted his head back, looked up and said in a monotonous and irritating tone, *"Why did I not say something sooner? Maybe if I had said something sooner this would not have happened, but they had no right to react like that. If only I had said something sooner. I reacted quickly enough when the situation came to light, but if only had said something sooner it wouldn't have happened. Why did I not say something sooner?"*

Paul went on for a few minutes, ranting like a madman. His face growing more amused as he continued until I wasn't sure if he could stop from laughing out loud. The repetitive nature of his dialog was quite disturbing. It sounded so familiar, and yet unnatural to hear out loud. I understood what he was demonstrating. Many times my internal voice would not let something rest, and would go over the same event again and again; occasionally giving me a break, only to quickly return to the same recurring thoughts.

I wondered if we would all sound crazy if others could hear our internal dialogue. Would we all be that scary person on the bus talking to themselves as if they were two distinct people? Is that why we find it so alarming in others, because those are the secret private thoughts we all have?

Paul finally stopped his pretend-raving. "You know what I mean?" he asked.

"Yes," I agreed, "though it doesn't always sound so obsessive and crazy as you made it sound. Sometimes it's extremely reasonable."

"True, what's interesting though is that our internal voice is a complete and utter liar. It does not always know what is going on in our own mind nor the world. In fact, I would argue the narrator hardly ever knows what is going on, though to us, it feels like it does! Its purpose is to make sense of the world, and if it can't, then it just makes stuff up."

Shocked, I looked at Paul. "What do you mean?" I stammered out, "Of course you know what you are doing!"

"Do you?"asked Paul seriously. "Let me give you two examples that may disturb you more. Then, let me propose a different understanding for you." He pointed to opposing sides of his head, "As you know, the brain has two separate hemispheres that are connected together by a bundle of neural fibers to carry communication between them. There is surgery that can be done to sever the connection between the two hemispheres of the brain. This actually results in what is termed a 'split brain'. Two completely functioning hemispheres that are no longer connected and that can no longer communicate with each other through their normal methods."

"Why would anyone do that?" I interjected, a little horrified at the thought of why such an operation would be carried out.

"Sadly, when a patient is suffering from an extreme case of epilepsy, it has been the only treatment that can stop the continuous seizures. It may be their only chance to have a somewhat normal life," he answered.

"A split brain is extraordinarily interesting to study from a neurologist's viewpoint because now the language center that is located on the left side is isolated from the right side of the brain. One of the functions of the language center is the vocalization of thoughts. Now, our left eye is not connected to the left hemisphere of the brain. It's connected to the right. So we have a situation where the information going through the left eye goes into the right hemisphere and can't get to the language center on the other side because the brain has been split.'

"Simply put, a person with a split brain has no ability to vocalize what is seen by the left eye because it never gets that information. To show this, researchers wrote a command on a piece of card and then placed it in such a position that the card was only visible to the subject's left eye. The command they wrote was '*Go get a drink from the fridge.*' On reading it, the subject would then stand up, go to the fridge and take out a drink. Sounds straightforward, right?"

I silently nodded.

"But if you interrupt them and ask them what they are doing or why they suddenly left the chair in the middle of the experiment, they don't know why! How can they, when their language center, cut off by the brain surgery, never received the information? Their narrator doesn't know why they are moving towards the fridge. But here is why it's especially fascinating. They don't answer 'I have no idea', they aren't puzzled by their own behavior. They completely fabricate a reasonable answer. Explaining that they wanted to stretch their legs or were feeling thirsty and decided to get a drink. They aren't consciously aware that they were commanded to go get a drink. Their narrator sees their behavior and makes up a plausible excuse for their behavior. They believe this explanation completely, but the explanation is not true!"

He finished his drink and paused to push it to the side so a passing waiter could pick it up, which gave me time to digest what he was saying. This was a bizarre scenario and obviously not a real life situation that he described. Still, why was the person not confused? Why were they so adamant about their false convictions? It was puzzling.

"The second experiment I want you to think about," his attention back on me, "was carried out way back in the 60s. It still has scientists and philosophers discussing the ramifications. In this experiment, a subject was asked to sit down and in his own time get up again. He was also asked to indicate exactly when he made the decision to stand up, so they knew when he consciously made the decision. The whole time he was being monitored by a device that registers activity in the brain. The results were surprising to the researchers. The subject indicated they were about to get up only a split second before they actually got up. The brain showed activity a full second before they got up."

Paul paused. "Do you understand what I'm saying?"

I thought I did. "You are saying that the decision to get up was made before the guy knew about it."

"Exactly!" Paul exclaimed, "Every time, it could be easily seen that brain activity started way before the subject declared he was going to get up. The researchers could predict with stunning accuracy when the subject would stand, even before he knew it himself. This is the reverse of what we would envision. We believe we make a conscious decision, and then instruct our body to get up.'

"So let me pose you some questions for thought. Who are you? Are you the brain that decides to get up, or the conscious mind that just reports you are getting up? Are you the brain that can drive a car by itself without attention, or the mind that daydreams while you are driving?" Paul stopped talking as loud music suddenly started. There was a lot of activity going on, and people were starting to form a large circle on the beach around someone. Paul indicated that the fire dancing was about to start, and he suggested we pause our chat until after the show.

We stood up, and from this position we were looking slightly down on the beach at the fire show. It gave us an exceptional viewpoint. I was sure Paul had known this, and it was why he had picked this particular table. I was grateful to my friend for thinking ahead. Strange that I was beginning to think of this man so quickly as my friend, but he had an unusually relaxed and friendly manner that was engaging.

The fire show was excellent. There were several different people who demonstrated their skills to music that had a fast beat. In one, a man had a staff lit on fire at both ends. He twirled it around and around his body, creating fire shapes in the night air; often throwing the staff far up into the night to be caught with one hand and then smoothly resuming his twirling dance. The show was great fun, and gave me a distraction from our intense discussion.

After the show ended, we returned to our seats. Paul thought it best we order food now, so after some consideration of the menus, we placed our orders and refreshed our drinks. Paul launched right in once the order was done.

"So, to summarize where we were. The brain has many specialized areas that act like a bunch of middle managers all jostling for attention, competing to be heard. Then we have the narrator, which I think of as the marketing manager of the company. The narrator keeps a story going, even if it has no idea what is going on in the departments. Its job is to make sure you feel like you know what's going on, like you have a sense of continuity from moment to moment."

I stopped him with a hand. "I'm sorry, I find this profoundly disturbing. You're essentially saying I don't know what is going on in my head. That I have no free will that..." I found myself lost for words for a second. "That I'm just a spin story made up by a marketing manager who lives in my brain."

"Yes and no. That is a particularly dramatic way of presenting it. However, you have summed up the dilemma the experimenters found themselves in. Do we have free will? Or do we just act and then make up a storyline for ourselves? There has always been a debate about free will among philosophers. I find philosophical arguments intriguing sometimes, but mostly exhausting and somewhat pointless. Current arguments that result from these experiments boil down to whether free will is just an illusion, or if the concept of free will even matters anyway. There are very few convincing arguments put forward by scientists arguing that free will does exist."

"Well, what do you believe?" I asked.

"Oh, I have no doubt free will exists!" he said. "None at all. At least in all the ways that matter."

"After all you have said? Why?"

"Because we can make the fundamental choices. I have no issue with someone expressing the concept that minute to minute we may be directed by our emotions and subconscious. However, we can make the larger decisions in life. We can direct and change those subconscious processes.'

"We can select how we wish to develop. We can direct and create our life. We can choose how we react to the difficulties that life throws at us. We can find those traits that we dislike in ourselves and change them. Our whole lives are a demonstration of free will. Even if most people seldom exercise it," he finished.

I mulled this over. It didn't sit right with me. I thought about my life. I was not happy with it. Otherwise, I wouldn't read all those 'fix it in ten minutes' self-help books. I thought grimly to myself that none of them had actually helped me anyway.

"I don't think I can totally agree with you that we can change ourselves, Especially behaviors we don't like in ourselves," I said slowly. "There are many facets of my life that I have tried to change," I paused then added a bit lamely, "and generally I failed."

"I never said it was easy," he laughed, "but it can be done. Like most people, you probably failed because you tried to do too much, or maybe too fast, or maybe you really didn't want to change enough."

Leaning forward, he looked at me intently.

"You can improve yourself, but only if you really commit to it. I can show you how." His tone was light but challenging.

"I would like that," I said.

"Good," he said. "Then we will start on how you can do it tomorrow."

Diving buddy and coral

5

Practice

"In the next few days, I'm going to try to show you how to change your general attitudes, while improving behaviors in those areas that you value and want to grow," said Paul.

Arching one eyebrow, I turned to him. "That's what I like about you, Paul, you don't promise much."

He laughed. "I can show you the methods, but in the end it's always you that has to do the work."

We were sitting at the end of the Infinity Bay dock next to the post where Paul practiced his handstands. Our feet dangled below the edge, just inches above the water. I could see hundreds of little tropical fish dart in and out of the shade. Paul said he liked to sit here early in the day and look back at the beach to remind himself why he lived here. I knew exactly what he meant. From here we could see the entire beach. White sands, palm trees and blue water. Perfect for any tropical postcard.

"First, I'd like you to understand how change happens in relation to time. Time can be your best friend or worst enemy. The moment we are born we start to grow and learn, and it never stops. At first, that growth is dictated by genes and our immediate circumstances. If we are lucky, we are born into a nurturing environment that facilitates both our character and intellectual development through parenting and schools. We are initially thrust out into the world following a path over which we have little influence.'"

Distracted, Paul pointed to a sudden swarm of bright yellow
fish that were swimming by in the water below. I watched them
until they disappeared out of view beneath us.

"I remember when I first decided to start doing handstands,"
he continued, "I hunted around until I found someone who could
do what I wanted to achieve. When I finally found him, he esti-
mated that starting from scratch, especially at my age, it would
take me three years at least to progress this far. It seemed like an
impossible task. I was daunted, and I expressed something of that
nature to him. He was unimpressed with my attitude. He then said
something that I have carried with me since that day."

"What was it he said?" I asked, intrigued.

"He asked me in a very serious tone if I planned to be alive
in three years. That question, for me, puts it all in perspective. You
see, our culture is so obsessed with immediate change. As if we
can change our character like turning on and off a light switch. It
took us many years to become the person we are now, and it takes
time to change ourselves into someone else. Some behaviors can
change overnight, of course. If something monumental happens
to you, a frightening life-changing event like a heart attack, then
you might change your lifestyle the very next day. Strong emotions
like fear can be extremely persuasive. But that is not the norm. If
you want to have lasting change in your life, then it's usually done
incrementally, and those tiny changes are initially invisible to those
around you.'

"We have, as a culture, started acting as if our ss is something to be achieved in the future. We put off living life today to
its fullest in the mistaken belief that some future goal or event
is going to make us happy. The fact is that humans are adaptive
creatures. Once a long sought after goal has been achieved, the latest toy purchased or life event accomplished, we may have a short
period of ss, but we soon adapt. Then we repeat the same behavior
as if the result will be different."

"But your handstands are goals too. Aren't goals just a way
of measuring our progress?" I argued.

"I prefer to call them milestones rather than goals. There is something finite about a goal I dislike, whereas a milestone is just a place passed on a journey."

"A journey to where?"

"That is up to each one of us," he said.

"The point I'm trying to make is that living is not a set of goals to be achieved, it's a process. Each and every moment is precious. If you live your life focused only on a distant point in the future, you will not be happy where it counts, which is right here and now. There may be a short burst of ss once you reach your goal, but our minds recalibrate quickly, adjusting to each new situation. So why do that to ourselves? Why not make sure you enjoy the journey first and foremost and just savor the milestones as they pass?"

"I'm sorry, but you sound a little self-contradictory. One moment you are telling me I need to focus on long term goals that can take three years or more, and the next you are saying I need to focus on the here and now. Which is it?"

"It's both," he joked, "I'm quite comfortable holding contradictory views on matters. I think it's healthy. But of course in reality, if managed well, they are not contradictory but complementary. You need to see where you want to be in the future. Or rather what you want to become. Then you can map out a way forward, but the goal is only beneficial to set the general direction. Taking joy in the day-to-day movement in that direction is key to lifelong ss.

"When I was asked to give the course at that recent conference, I struggled to decide exactly what to talk about. I tried to distill what I wanted to convey into some short sessions based around what I decided to call *foundation principles*. These are basic principles, that if we understand and accept, are meant to help us build the positive changes we all want in our lives."

"What were they?"

"I'm going to go through them all if I can before you leave. We have just been talking about the first one"

˙He held up one finger. "Number One: Conscious Growth. We have no choice about changing; as we grow older it continues regardless of our wishes. The person you are now is not the person you are going to be in two years, five years or ten years. So you can either grow arbitrarily, or you can grow with purpose in the direction you choose.'

"What I'm going to show you in the next few days is nothing particularly new - it's gleaned from experimentation, science, and even from various faiths. But all of it works. If we had more time, I would go into a lot of details, especially the science behind it, but now I just want to make sure you understand the core principles and practices. Okay?"

I nodded my understanding.

"As I explained earlier, to change a behavior permanently you probably need thirty days of doing it every single day. We don't have that much time together, but that's not what's important. You have more than thirty days with yourself - you have the rest of your life."

Looking out to sea where the reef broke the surface of the water, I reflected on what he was saying. It made perfect sense. I had never actually thought about it in such simple terms, and I did plan to be around for a lot more than three years.

"Today we are going to cover general conditioning. In physical exercise, this would be akin to aerobic exercise or maybe yoga. It's something you need to do every day to keep your mind in good condition. Making it work for you and not against you. Yesterday we talked about the part of our brain called the narrator, do you remember what we said about it?"

"Yes," I replied, "the narrator is our inner voice. It's the one that runs the dialogs in our head. It helps us find meaning, but it's quite capable of lying to us," I paused and turned my head to look at him. "I'm still really uncomfortable with that. I thought about it a lot last night. The idea that I might not know what I'm doing feels very wrong."

Paul thoughtfully nodded his head as he turned to my gaze.

"Yes, it's a disturbing thought. It has been troubling many people since the evidence showed that we know about our actions after the fact. But I think they might be looking at it completely wrong."

"Why do you say that?" I asked.

"A lot of scientists spend their time dividing and separating the brain into functional areas and then studying those areas. It's valuable research. It tells us how the brain works in particular respects, but they all agree that the mind is more than the sum of its parts. Yet when it comes to the narrator, our inner voice, it's often discussed as if it's actually the complete person not just another part of the mind."

"Well it's me. I think, therefore I am and all that."

"No, I think that is the wrong perspective. The narrator is just a part of our mind like any other part. It serves its purpose, which is to do a different kind of thinking. When do you really use your internal dialog? We use it to solve problems that our mind can't do unconsciously. We use it especially when we want to reason out the future," he said.

I thought about it for a few seconds and about our talk yesterday. "I guess I use it when I need to think something through carefully. It could be a task I need to do or how to approach a problem. In addition, as we discussed, it can be a reminder or a nag about disturbing situations."

"But isn't that also solving a problem?" he interjected. "When you replay a situation over and over in your mind, aren't you essentially trying to solve it? Trying to make it palatable, so it goes away."

"Yes," I agreed after a little thought. "I guess once it becomes solved or I'm at peace with it, I can drop it. Then the dialog diminishes and eventually disappears."

"Think also of how it's possible to drive a car without conscious attention, but if we run into danger or something novel that needs attention, we are yanked back to awareness. In essence, it's called in to solve a problem."

"So you are saying that the narrator is just a problem solver," I said.

"It's an extremely sophisticated problem solver," he said emphasizing the word 'extremely', "but it's still only a part of your mind. A part that is called in when it's needed and should depart when it's not. It seems to have become established in society that our inner voice defines who we are. Probably because we use it when we do higher level thinking. When in fact, sometimes it's just an annoying marketing manager for your brain that won't shut up.'

"Think about it next time you have a conversation with someone. Do you consciously think through each reply? No, especially if the conversation is moving quickly. What comes out of your mouth can sometimes be a surprise. The phrase *I can't believe I just said that* is just the narrator backtracking on a comment that does not fit into its current story."

It seemed so obvious to me that this voice echoing in my head was fully engaged. "I still feel like it's me," I said stubbornly.

"I understand," said Paul. "Have you ever asked yourself who the voice is talking to or is it really a one-sided conversation?"

"Well, me." I pointed to myself.

"Exactly," he said, "and if you said aloud what you internally said to yourself so that everyone could hear? What do you think they would think about you?"

"They would think I was off my rocker, some kind of escaped mental patient," I answered, having already considered that point.

"Yes they would, but why? We all have that voice in our heads. It's fascinating that talking to yourself in your head is acceptable but talking out loud to yourself is considered utterly crazy." He held up his hand. "That's not really important to our discussion. My belief is that your inner voice is just another part of your brain. It's not the whole of you, and you should have it under control."

Shifting a little restlessly on the dock, he held up two fingers. "My second foundation is simple. *You can't control what happens to you, so condition yourself on how to react.* That way, whatever happens, you are ready."

"I'm going to show you three types of meditation today. You are going to have to set time aside to do them every day if you want them to help. It can be any time of the day that's convenient for you. None of them takes a long time."

Meditation. I screwed up my face a little as I had hoped for something more dramatic. Paul must have seen my look out of the corner of his eye, a slight grin tugged at the corner of his lips.

"What we are about to do is necessary. It will calm you. It has many health benefits: it reduces stress, blood pressure, inflammation, boosts immunity, and even fertility. I promise that I'm not making these facts up. Long term studies have shown these medical benefits. If that is not enough, I'm sure they make you into a happier person. More likable and compassionate as well. Can you get those benefits with any medication around today?"

"No," I said, "you can't."

"And sitting on the end of a dock is as good a place to learn as any. Have you done any meditation before?"

I explained to him that I had tried before and experienced problems trying to clear my mind.

"Not a problem. Most people tend to overcomplicate the process. I just want you to sit in an upright position. Place your hands on your lap, and when you are comfortable, close your eyes." Shifting my weight on the dock, I tried to sit upright. "How long are we going to do this for?" I asked, feeling more than a little self-conscious.

"We have only just started, and you want it to end," he said seriously. "Well, the Dalai Lama does it for more than six hours a day, but I don't think we should aim that high to start with. How about two hours?"

I turned my head and stared at him in horror. He could *not* be serious. I was not going to sit at the end of the dock for two hours. After a second or two, his expression collapsed, and he grinned.

"You deserved that after the '*how long*' remark. Not exactly the strongest commitment I have seen in my life."

Mollified, I returned to relaxing in an upright position. I took a deep breath and closed my eyes.

"We are going to do this for about ten minutes, and then we are going to do something else for the last five minutes. By then the sun will be getting too hot to stay sitting out here. Now to start,

I just want you to close your eyes and breathe in and out through your nose. Take long deep breaths, observe your breath as you do so and relax. Notice your breathing without concentrating on it. Just notice it. The technique in this meditation is *not to try*. Don't try to clear your mind. Your narrator is going to have lots of stuff to talk to you about. In fact, more than normal, it might seem. But that's probably because you are used to there being a lot of external distractions. Whenever you find your mind moving to a train of thought, just notice it and bring your attention back gently to your breathing. Don't force it. Just notice it and return to the breath. You are probably going to do this back and forth for the whole ten minutes. It's not an issue.'

"Just breathe, and if you notice you are distracted, return to the breath," he repeated.

After those words he became very quiet. From the moment we started, my mind wandered again and again. Sometimes the noises around me grabbed my attention, the lapping of the water, the sound of a boat passing. Other times, my mind generated thoughts. Thoughts about food, diving, my time with Paul, what I was doing here. It didn't matter how many times I returned to my breathing, I just kept getting distracted. At first, I jerked my mind back to the breathing, but then realized I was trying too hard, so I just noticed I was distracted and focused on my breath. Often my mind went straight back to the same thought.

After what seemed like ages, Paul spoke again. "That's about ten minutes. I just wanted to show you how it works and experience it. Any questions?"

I explained my problems.

"That's normal, don't worry about it. I think many people give up meditation too quickly because they think they are doing it wrong. Try to do that for ten or twenty minutes a day for thirty days, and it will become easier. You will still find yourself easily distracted, but that is fine. I strongly recommend you get some books on meditation or take a class, as I just scratched the surface. However, that is the essence of it. After time, the voice will quiet ,and you will find that the calmness you begin to experience carries over to the rest of the day. The more you progress, the more benefits you will feel. You are stilling both your body and mind; learning to relax, slow down and detach yourself."

It was becoming hot sitting in the sun, and he suggested we find some shade. Heading down the dock and onto the beach, he led the way to a row of deck chairs that were immediately in front of the hotel. The guard nodded to him, obviously recognizing him, and Paul gestured for me to lie in one of the chairs.

"Just relax and we will start the second form of meditation."

I made myself comfortable on the chair as he continued talking.

"We touched on this form already when I showed you how to remove pain and obsession yesterday. This type of meditation will affect the way you interact with others. Practicing this on a daily basis will make you far more compassionate and forgiving. It will also allow you to move past the petty squabbles that are a natural part of our interaction with others.'

"I want you to close your eyes and think about something or someone that is easy to love, like a child. Just as you did before. See yourself sending love to them. Feel the sensations of doing it. Once you are comfortable, we are going to rotate people in and out of your visualization, starting with those closest to you like friends and family members. Then if we have time, we will move on to acquaintances and strangers. We are going to do this for about five to ten minutes."

He asked me to close my eyes, and once again he talked me through the process. I remembered the basic technique from the coffee shop, so I quickly got the idea. I relaxed and summoned up my little nephew and surrounded him with a visible light filled with unconditional love. Then after a few seconds, I replaced him with another member of my family. I dwelled a little longer on some members of my family, as I thought they needed some extra love. After I had moved through my family, I started going through my friends. By the time Paul called a stop, I had moved on to some work colleagues.

"Okay, you can open your eyes now," he said.

I did. In the warmth of the day, lying on the beach chair, I felt extremely relaxed. Looking up at Paul, I asked him to explain exactly why we were doing these two meditations.

"There are many reasons why meditation is a good practice to have in your life; I have already mentioned the health benefits, but let me give you my reasons. Do you remember how we talked at the beginning about ingraining habits by practicing them again and again? By practicing them we create an easy path for our mind to travel along. The brain loves to take the simple route."

"Yes I remember," I said.

"During the day we are constantly creating those paths, regardless of whether we like it or not. Often laying them with worry, concern or other negative emotions. We can easily create patterns of thought that lock us into repeating destructive behaviors. Since all the emotions like stress, fear, anger and so on affect our biochemistry, we are also effecting the health of our body. By meditating, we are affectively giving our brain a chance to detach ourselves from those paths. By letting the thoughts go without emotion, and by returning to the calming breath when we experience disturbances, we are calming the mind and retraining it to work the way we want it to work. By relaxing, we allow our body's chemistry to return to a normal or non-stressed state."

"That makes a lot of sense. So I'm effectively unlearning the bad practices I create throughout the day. Following your logic, my guess is that the goal of the second meditation is to actively practice some new paths but this time consciously lay them down in a positive manner."

Paul beamed at me. "Exactly! It's not enough to unlearn and detach yourself from the bad paths; it's necessary to condition the brain to do what we want it to do. By directing our thoughts in a compassionate manner, we will find it becoming more and more evident in our daily behavior."

"But these are very general behaviors. What about if I want to mend a specific character flaw I have?"

Paul arched an eyebrow. "Like impatience? You are jumping ahead, we will look at that later. For now, let's go and get something to eat."

After a little discussion, we decided to eat right here at the Infinity Bay Resort. There was some shade from the palm trees, and we could still see the beach. The sea was so still that not even the reef was causing a ripple on the surface. The only movement was caused by water taxis going back and forth to the restaurants of West End.

We ordered breakfast. While eating, we discussed our plans for the day. I, of course, was planning to get in my normal two dives. With only a few days left on my trip, I didn't want to miss a single one. Paul was heading over to West End for the rest of the day with some visiting friends. He suggested we meet over there after my dives at a bar called Sundowners to watch the sunset. It sounded like a great idea.

Paul had ordered a small fruit salad with his breakfast but hadn't touched it. He now placed it in front of me and pushed it towards me.

"Now it's time for your last lesson this morning," he said, motioning to the fruit bowl.

"Fruit salad?" I said with a questioning look on my face.

"Exactly that," he said. "The first meditation you did teaches you to calm the mind and maintain a sense of detachment, the second helps you develop compassion in your daily life, and this final one will help you live totally in the moment. To enjoy and savor each second, rather than living in the future or the past, which is what we tend to do."

Pushing the bowl directly in front of me, he continued. "First, you can do this anywhere, anytime. It's a matter of being able to slow down and savor a moment in time. I want you to pick up a piece of fruit from the bowl, but I want you to be aware of all your senses as you do it, cataloging the experience. What does each piece feel like in your hand? Is it wet or dry, smooth or rough? How does the texture feel between your fingers? How does it respond to a little pressure? Then look at it carefully, minutely. What color is it, does the color vary, how? Explore it with your eyes, looking at every detail. Don't rush, but examine it carefully, then smell it. How does it smell? Is the smell strong, or faint? Place it in your mouth and notice the experience as you let it sit there, and then explore the fruit with your tongue. Feel the texture as you play with it. Taking your time, bite into it or apply pressure to it. Constantly notice any change in texture or taste as you do so. Then move to chewing it - experience the change of consistency, taste, texture, or temperature. Finally, swallow it and notice if the taste lingers or fades in your mouth. Notice the movement of your tongue, mouth and throat in the swallowing process. When you are done, choose a different piece of fruit and repeat the process. Don't rush. Just be an intimate observer of all you do and experience. Enjoy every movement and sensation. I will be back in a few minutes. Enjoy the fruit."

With that, he pushed back his chair and left, walking over to the bar where he struck up a conversation with one of the staff who he obviously knew quite well.

My eyes returned to the fruit bowl. I understood what the meditation was about. There was a large movement about *being in the now* in the media. The idea that we tend to drift through our lives without paying attention was not a new one, but I didn't realize there were exercises to focus your attention in the *now*.

I picked up a piece of fruit at random. It felt strange, as normally I would've used a fork. Between my fingers was a piece of melon. It was wet to the touch, and I instinctively started to put it into my mouth. Consciously stopping, I told myself, 'This is supposed to be a slow and measured activity.' I made myself think slowly and deliberately. I noticed how it felt slippery between my fingers and how the juice was slowly gathering at one corner as I held it. I noticed the color was a golden yellow which had a hint of green at the edge. I realized it must have been cut close to the outside of the melon. I raised it to my nose, breathed in its delicate fragrance, and noticed the exact distance at which I could smell it.

I put it against my lips. It felt cold, like it had just come from a fridge. I noticed the way my mouth was already salivating, anticipating the sweetness. Placing it gingerly in my mouth, I enjoyed the rush of syrupy taste. I touched it with my tongue. How different it felt to my tongue than to my fingers. Cool, wet and sweet. I savored its taste. Biting down, I enjoyed the way the fruit released juice and noticed it was more watery than I had expected. I slowly chewed it, enjoying the coolness and the way the melon came apart in my mouth. Swallowing it, I observed my muscles working together to move it down, and how my mouth seemed to feel regret at its absence.

It was strange to think that one piece of fruit could give you so much pleasure. It reminded me of how people would eat their first spoon of ice cream out of a bowl, slowly and savoring the taste.

I looked around. Paul was still engaged in conversation. I took another piece, cataloging each sensation as it occurred. It took me about ten minutes to finish a fruit cup that would normally have taken a minute. When I had finished, I pushed the empty bowl to the center of the table and then stared at it

A strange feeling of regret washed through me. Not because I had finished the fruit. By the end, the sensations were dulling as if my brain needed newer stimuli. Even the tastiest foods are boring in excess.

No, I was thinking about the breakfast I had just eaten. I had been engrossed in my conversation with Paul and hardly remembered what I had swallowed. There had been fruit, toast and jelly. I had no real memory of the taste. I wondered how many simple pleasures I missed by being too busy to notice them. How many moments had I missed by not focusing my attention on them?

Paul came back to the table. Sitting down, he looked at me and asked me how it had been. I thought for a time before I answered.

"Good," I answered.

"Good," he repeated.

"Yes, good," I said thoughtfully.

Paul waited patiently for me to say more.

"The fruit tasted as good as anything I have ever tasted before. I'm wondering if all food would taste as good if I took the time to notice."

"No, probably not. I deliberately chose something that would be fun and tasty. But taking the time to savor your food is never a bad idea. Of course, this was just an exercise and could be applied to any task you perform. Even something as mundane as sweeping the kitchen floor can be interesting if you try to experience it to its fullest."

I thought about that. What sensations would that give me? The feel of the broom in my hand. What kind of material is it: cold metal, warm wood? Is it smooth or rough? What does it look like? How does the pressure against my hands feel as I move the brush? What a strange train of thought. The idea of cataloging the experience made me want to try it. Very strange.

"What is important is to take five to ten minutes a day to truly experience something you are doing. To savor it. To notice each and every sensation," he said.

"I assume by training my mind to do this, the practice spreads into other parts of my life?" I asked.

"Yes it does. It's astonishing how much more you can enjoy life and be happier if you actually practice *enjoying the now* by experiencing it to its fullest."

"Time to go. I will see you at 5:30, at Sundowners in West End." He put some money on the table to pay for his food and quickly left.

As I reviewed the check, I wondered about what we had done today. It was not the first time I had attempted meditation. Before, it had always been couched in more spiritual terms. Paul seemed to see all he showed me as exercises that develop the mind with a clear understanding of the benefits. Obviously he saw his mind as no different from his body. He had worked hard to condition his body for handstands, and similarly, he worked hard to condition his mind for happiness.

Hunting Lionfish

6

Focus

The journey from West Bay to West End only takes 10 minutes in one of the many water taxis that spend their day ferrying tourists back and forth. West Bay, with its hotels and long white beach, is a popular destination during the day, whereas West End, with its bars and restaurants, draws them out in the evening. The boats hug the shore on the inside of the reef, moving at a fast pace but slow enough to enjoy looking back at the jungle reaching to the water's edge.

I arrived a little early in West End, about an hour before sunset. It has a long concrete road with gentle twists and turns from one end to the other as it follows the shore. The waterside alternates between small sandy beaches and bars with long docks projecting over the water. The taxi dropped me only a few minutes' walk from Sundowners, where I was supposed to meet Paul. I stretched out the time a little by doing a meandering walk between the shops selling tourist gifts and peering into the bars and restaurants as I passed. I remembered one bar called the Blue Marlin vividly from the night before, and I guessed that the street would soon be swarming with happy people out to enjoy the evening.

Sundowners is one of the oldest still-operational bars on Roatan, and is really not much more than a large square wooden shack situated on the beach side of the West End Road. The four sides of the square are lined with stools, trapping the bartenders inside. It's not the age or look of Sundowners that makes it so popular. It's ideally situated in the middle of Half Moon Bay, and from any spot at the bar you're constantly aware you're on a beautiful Caribbean island. Popular with locals and tourists alike, it's always crowded at sunset.

Paul was standing at the bar drinking a beer with a group of noisy individuals. I walked up to the bar and ordered a drink for myself, then stood in his field of view not wanting to intrude yet hoping to be noticed. After a few minutes, Paul looked up from his conversation, saw me, and quickly made his excuses. He moved through the crowd at the bar to where I was standing.

"One of the problems and joys of living in such a small community is everywhere you go you're surrounded by people you know. Sundowners is a big local hangout," he said, gesturing to his friends. Pointing to some chairs far away from the noise of the bar, he added, "Let's move over there so we can chat while we watch the sun go down. Good day diving?"

"Yes, great. It amazes me how many different dive sites are here. You could dive for months and not visit them all. Do you dive yourself?"

"I used to dive a lot, but I've gotten out of the habit in recent years. I go sometimes with my friends from Coconut Tree Divers across the street. I must admit, your enthusiasm has piqued my interest again, and I think I see some dives in my near future. Let's talk before we watch the sunset; I think we have about 15 minutes."

He glanced over his shoulder, looking at the sun. A group of tourists were standing not far behind us at the water's edge. They were taking turns shooting photos of each other. Each one of them stood by the water holding a variety of different poses, each position included them holding their hand out flat to the side. After each photo they would all run back into a group, review it, and then cheer in excitement.

"What on earth are those people doing?" I said, indicating the tourists.

Paul watched them for a for a good while, seemingly lost in

thought. Finally he pointed to the sun.

"You see where the sun is now. They're trying to take photos so that the setting sun is part of their pose. It will give the illusion that the sun is resting on their hand. It's a lot of fun and makes for enjoyable photos."

My curiosity satisfied, I returned my attention to him. "Sorry, you were saying?"

"Yes. Let's talk before the sun starts to set. You asked me earlier today when I was showing you the meditation how you could improve specific behaviors. I will show you a method for doing that tomorrow, but I think it's important to first discuss focus and how it directly affects our growth and happiness."

"Okay."

"What we pay attention to in life will significantly adjust how we feel and also how we deal with life. It's difficult to control where and how we focus, but it's an important discipline to master."

"I'm not sure I understand. We focus on whatever is the matter at hand and what we need to do to get through the day. At least, that's what I do. I focus on my work when I'm working, I focus on my diving when I'm diving. Agreed, my mind wanders. It even daydreams sometimes, but I hardly feel that's such a big issue. I can usually master it and get back to what's at hand. Especially if it's important."

He listened and said, "You're right in terms of focusing on an actual process. But what I'm talking about is more about how we deal with the difficulties in our daily lives. And how we deal with and feel about those difficulties is dictated mostly by how we focus on them. Let me give you a thought experiment to show you what I mean."

"Sure," I said, nodding my agreement.

"I want you to turn your head and look at all the people in the bar, and tell me how many of them are wearing swimsuits?"

It seemed pretty straightforward. I quickly scanned my eyes over all the patrons sitting and standing at the bar. Many were still wearing just a swimsuit. I quickly scanned the area, adding them all up and came to 15, give or take a few who I thought blurred the line between swimsuits and clothes.

I turned back to Paul and announced my answer, "15, approximately."

Holding my gaze with his eyes he said, "Very good. Now without looking back at the bar, tell me how many people were barefooted, how many had hats on, and what would you say are the most predominant colors of the guys' swimsuits?"

His eyebrows arched at the consternation on my face. I should've known there would be more to his experiment. I tried to visualize the bar, the people standing around it. I was sure I had seen a few that were barefooted, but I could not place where they were at the bar. I had not looked at their heads and could not hazard a guess at how many hats were being worn. As for the swimsuit colors, my mind could only recall one very attractive lady in a blue bikini. I could not remember any of the guys at all.

He let me stammer my way through an attempt to sum up what I remembered, which was hardly anything, before he laughed and let me off the hook.

"It's okay. I don't actually need the details. I'm more interested in you thinking about what you actually did there," he said. "Go ahead and take a look if you like."

Feeling a small sense of relief, I looked around at the bar. It was actually embarrassing how wrong I was. I realized I had just started fabricating answers, as I hadn't noticed the details. I had assumed most of the people still in swimsuits were barefooted. They were not. I could only see one person barefooted. Most wore flip-flops or casual sandals. Very few hats of any kind were in evidence. The beautiful girl was the only one wearing blue.

I turned back to Paul. "I guess you're going to point out that since I was focused on the swimsuits I wasn't paying attention to everything else."

He nodded. "Partially, yes. I admit, I chose a subject matter that I thought might draw your attention. But when we're specifically looking for something, we often fail to notice other things that are right in front of our eyes. Sometimes this is useful, allowing us to carry on a task without distractions, but in general it's not.

If we have preconceived ideas about an experience then that will often taint the whole experience."

"So you're saying that it would be better to have some kind of Zen-like open mind, so that we are open to anything."

"Well, that would be great, but very few people walk around like that. It's far simpler to accept the fact that we have this quirk and use it in a positive and constructive way."

"How?"

"When I was younger, I had a career in sales. I went to many different types of sales trainings, but one item always came out as being very important. *If you're the one asking the questions then you control the sales process.* That goes from the cheesy closing lines that retail sales people have been known to use such as, 'How would you like to pay for that, cash or charge?' The sentence of course assumes that you're buying an item and have just moved onto how you're going to pay for it. There are more sophisticated selling techniques, in which the salesperson asks you questions to elicit information about your business. By thoroughly understanding your business, he can discover problems that he might be able to solve with his product. Even though they differ greatly on a scale of sophistication, they're essentially the same technique. In each, a salesperson is directing your thoughts to the areas they want by asking you questions."

"Now what if you became your own salesperson, deliberately directing your thoughts? Knowing that your focus and thoughts can be directed, you continually asked yourself the questions that lead you to where you want your thoughts to be?"

"Yesterday, my narrator was a marketing manager, and now I'm a salesperson. You are making turning my mind into a business, Paul."

He shrugged. "We use the concepts we're familiar with, and I spent my life doing business. Let me give you some crude examples. If you wake up in the morning and ask yourself to list all the good things that are going to happen to you and all the things you're going to achieve today, do you think you will be in a different frame of mind than if you just get up and list the problems you have to take care of today? Or if something goes wrong in your day, what will be the difference in how you feel if you think about it more in terms of what you can learn and how you can grow from the experiences, rather than dwell on the pain or irritation caused by the day's incidents?"

"Oh, you mean positive thinking," I said.

"Yes and no. I'm not a believer in positive thinking in the sense where you just try and put a rosy outlook on everything, and worse still, believe that if you just think positive thoughts that everything will turn out well. Because in reality, just wishing something would happen has absolutely no effect on the outcome."

"You know a lot of people are going to disagree with you there, Paul! There are some awfully popular books out there with a lot of followers who believe that you can attract things into your life just by thinking positively about them."

Paul sighed. "Yes, I know that. I believe in a positive and empowering mental attitude, if the result of that attitude is to get you to take some action. I do not believe that what goes on in your head affects the world one iota unless you do something."

Paul started to sip his drink, as I said with a straight face, "Maybe that's why they're rich and famous and you aren't."

Paul convulsed and practically spit out part of his drink as he started to laugh uncontrollably.

Laughing, I said, "I think that gets you back for my first night!"

Paul stammered out, "I think you're right! I might point out in my own defense, it's the authors of those books that got rich and not necessarily the people who read them. Though by the law of large numbers, if enough people read the books then some of them are going to get rich regardless. Which would give them some good results. If I can get back to my point before your rude and funny interruption?"

I inclined my head.

"I do believe in a positive and constructive attitude, and I believe it can be obtained by asking yourself empowering questions. It's one of the foundation principles for my talks: *Frame the situation correctly and ask empowering questions.* Just as you should have plans about where you want to be in the future, simply because the future will arrive regardless. Well, similarly, life is going to put you into a variety of situations that challenge you, so lay the groundwork and methodology of a positive and constructive approach to those situations ahead of time. Don't let circumstances and random situations dictate the direction of your thoughts. Better to practice asking yourself empowering questions rather than leave it to fate. That way, it becomes second nature to you when you really need it."

"I'm noticing a theme in our conversations. You seem to be constantly training the mind to certain ends. Exercising it almost."

"Yes, you have it. Like an athlete trains his body, like a fighter trains his reactions, like a gymnast practices their routines. Each is making a conscious decision to train to have their body react in a certain way. They consciously train it day in and day out so that whenever its needed, their body is ready. If they didn't, it wouldn't perform when they need it to. The mind is no different. In fact training the body is just a subset of training the mind. To train your body, you have to focus your mind, pay close attention to what you do. The body and the mind will still develop and grow without training, just not in the way you would probably choose or desire.'

"Remember my first foundation. *Conscious growth.* You can do this by making the time to meditate in order to give yourself a certain sense of detachment. Practice sending love to train a sense of compassion and forgiveness. Practice mindfulness to learn to savor and enjoy the moment. And ask the right questions to develop a sense of power and control in your own life."

"You haven't explained what you mean by the right questions?"

"Yes, you're right. Let's take a few different scenarios, and look at how you might choose to approach them: You have an argument with a friend you have known for a long time. He has stepped over some serious boundary and done something that was damaging to your relationship. You feel hurt and let down. It would be natural to dwell on it. Feeling upset may even be an appropriate emotion. What kind of questions could you ask yourself to help move forward in a positive way? What do you think?"

He indicated that I should speak. I thought about how I could try to move my thoughts in a good direction. "I could ask myself if they had a reason. Maybe I did something that created the situation?" I said.

Paul seemed to consider my answer. "That is a good question. A question that you should always be asking yourself in any situation where a problem has arisen in your life. But I'm not trying to make us always the focus or the cause of our problems, either. It might be better to ask ourselves if this is a unique situation? If it is, then ask ourselves how many times has this person been there to help us in the past? Remind ourselves about all the good times that we've had together. Any help they have given us when we needed it. Try to give yourself a sense of perspective. Maybe ask how we can let the person know that we had a problem with this incident without further damaging the relationship and if possible mending it.'

"One of the things I often notice is how we throw our past away for the strong emotions of the immediate present, and how we damage our futures as well by emphasizing the issue in front of us now. If we can repair this issue with our friend, how many more good times will we have together?"

"I see your point," I said.

"Let me give you some more general questions that might give you a better understanding. You could ask yourself these questions through the day:

How can I enjoy this more?
How can I help this person?
How can I improve how I handled that?
What can I learn from this?"

"I generally suggest that questions that start with a why are not very empowering. Questions such as 'why did this happen?' are not helpful. They direct our minds into a negative perspective because they're not really answerable. But our minds will try and answer them since we posed the question. This is at the core of what I'm trying to explain. Your mind will always be generating thoughts. All I'm saying is that you need to be the one directing them, not be at their mercy. If you ask those debilitating *why* questions or let your mind drift, the narrator is quite happy to make up answers and the answers it creates will neither be helpful nor empowering."

"By using '*how*' questions, we cause our mind to generate answers that are practical and helpful to our development. Now, just to show you that I'm not a positive thinker," he said with an amused look on his face, "there is one time when I think it's genuinely helpful to think of bad situations and direct your mind down that path."

"When?" I asked.

"I think to be truly happy you have to develop a certain sense of detachment. To realize that possessions and goals are outside of you and can be lost and replaced. Often, unhappiness can come because of fear of the unknown, fear of the future. Sometimes we just need to face down that fear to understand that even though we have a right to be concerned, our fear is out of proportion to reality. For instance, we are often terrified of taking risks because if we fail, we feel the consequences will be dire. Or we are unhappy in the course our lives have taken us, but the fear of the unknown is more frightening than living an unhappy life. In reality, there are few things worse than living an unhappy life.'

"In cases like these where you know you need to make changes, I feel the best course of action is to stare down our fears. It's seldom as bad a scenario as your imagination has created. Let me be clear on what I mean here by '*stare down our fears.*' We get so fearful of change, but if we really step through the consequences of our actions and break them down into pieces, they're not as terrible as we believe. So if I have some big project I'm working on, I sit down and think through the consequences of not doing it, and the negative consequences of doing it. Often my fears are more based on a fear of failure. Once you realize that the world will not end if you fail, it's far easier to move forward."

"Surely we do that anyway? If we dread something, don't we

constantly think about it?" I asked.

"No, worry is not the same as actually pulling apart the consequences of an action and thinking out the worst case scenario. Let me give you an example. Maybe you want to start a business, but you will need to quit your job to do it. Which will mean giving up a secure income, gambling on the success of the business, and potentially losing all your savings. It's possible that even though you have thought it through carefully, you can't make the final leap of faith. You keep procrastinating because you have a fear of losing everything.'

"But if you sit down and think it through, and clearly imagine all the worst case scenarios—and I do not mean imagine yourself starving to death on the streets—you can learn a lot. The point is to go through and say to yourself 'What if it doesn't work? What if I cannot get customers? What if I run out of money, what will I do?' If you think about it realistically, the worst situation is you will have to look for a job again, and you will have to start saving again. Yes, it may set you back, but you won't starve. You will survive. Some employers may even find the experience you gained worthwhile in future employment. If you think through the process, then you won't be so scared of the risks. Also, it's good to extend it to your current situation. You think your job is secure, but how secure is it? Companies have problems too. You may not be aware of them. Many people have gone to their jobs content in the security of their employment, only to leave that day carrying their stuff in a box because of company changes they didn't know were happening."

"That sounds really depressing," I said. "Don't you think looking for problems where none exists is going to make people more anxious?"

"I'm not saying invent problems just for the sake of it. Humans are terrible at predicting the future. They're also terrible at predicting their own emotional feelings in the future. We tend to think that we know what we feel like, but it's been shown again and again that we are both a bad judge of what we felt like in the past and a terrible judge of how we will feel in the future. Most people would predict that a year after winning the lottery they would be much happier than a year after losing a limb in an accident. The fact is, studies show we adjust in both situations. It's in our nature to adapt to situations, and we're good at it. In most cases, you will have moved on from an emotionally traumatic event within months. In time, the incident ceases to even factor into your present happiness. The phrase 'time heals all wounds' has a basis in fact."

I sat, a little stunned at this revelation. Could I eventually feel equally as happy, regardless of whether I had won the lottery or lost a limb? It seemed ridiculous, but I felt there must be some truth in what Paul said. I had heard many lottery winners say it hadn't made them happier, and knew that people who had lost limbs went on to lead happy and full lives. But it still felt wrong to me to even put those two events on a par.

"It doesn't seem possible to me that what you're saying is correct. No matter how many times I have heard that money doesn't make you happy, I believe that I would be happier winning the lottery!"

"Remember, I'm not saying that you aren't going to be happy about the event. Just that neither event is indicative of how happy you will be in the years to come. The fact that you feel that way is normal, and it demonstrates what we know about human behavior: we can't correctly predict happiness in the future. Sometimes to understand what I'm saying it's better to think about it another way. If someone has a tragic accident and loses a limb, do you think that means they can never be as happy as everyone else? Or if someone wins the lottery, does that mean they will always be happier than everyone else for the rest of their lives? No, to both questions. We adjust back to the norm.'

"As for money not being able to make you happy, it's totally true, once a certain level of subsistence has been met. Extra income does not make people happier. Something most people would not believe either. But still true, nevertheless while money doesn't make you happier, spending money on others can. If you use your money on helping others and giving gifts, it actually does increase your happiness. So past a certain point, it's not about how much money you have in life but how you use it that is important."

The bar was getting crowded, and the sun's approaching dip into the sea was almost upon us. Paul and I had finished our drinks while we were talking.

"There are so many people I know here - it's going to be hard to continue our conversation," he said as his eyes swept the bar full of noisy and happy people.

"Let's move to the restaurant next door. I have a table reserved for later, but we can go early, as I want to talk about your homework for tomorrow. Sundowners is a fun bar, but right now I think a little quieter might be better for us."

Paul led me away from the bar and into a large yellow wooden house next door. Up a staircase all but hidden in the middle of the house, which opened up onto a small deck with tables and chairs. A sign on the left read 'Welcome to the Landing'. The bar was still busy, but a lot quieter. Paul quickly moved to the only empty table which had 'Reserved' signs on it.

"Good, we're lucky," he said.

The bar, like Sundowners, had great views of Half Moon Bay, but from our slightly higher vantage point we could see up and down the beach both ways. The setting sun was perfectly framed by the two sides of the bay.

We ordered some drinks and settled in to watch the sunset.

"Have you ever seen a green flash at sunset?" I asked jokingly.

"Yes I have," he said seriously. "About eight times now, out of hundreds of sunsets."

"Really," I was surprised. "I thought the green flash was a myth from the movies."

"Yes, so did I when I arrived on the island. But I did some research, and it's just an optical effect that happens when all the conditions are right. You either have to be very lucky or watch a lot of sunsets to see one. I've watched a lot of sunsets!"

The sun was beginning to touch the water now, and I watched it with a hungry attention that did not invite interruption. There were very few clouds in the sky tonight, but there were some at the horizon, as the sun dipped down, it hid behind them, and the bright orange disk never actually seemed to touch the water; it just disappeared behind the distant clouds.

"You never see a flash if there are clouds at the horizon," remarked Paul. "It's only visible in the last second as the sun drops below the horizon. But here every sunset is beautiful." He gestured back to the horizon, and now that the sun had disappeared the sky was turning red and orange, and the few clouds in the sky were lit up by a sun that was now beyond our vision.

"I never tire of that," he said contentedly, turning back to face me. "I try to watch the sunrise and sunset every day, and here in the tropics it's not that hard to do since they're usually about twelve hours apart.'

"Tonight I want you to think about specific behaviors you would like to change. I want you to come up with a list of some character traits that you would like to change in yourself. Or I should say, that you would like to improve in yourself. They may be general traits, but they must be actionable. What I mean is, it's not enough to say 'I want to be a better person.' You need to answer the question: How, or in what way, do you want to be better? To be better has no specific meaning, but you could say 'I would like to be more generous.' Generosity is actionable. You could take action in several ways, from buying someone an unexpected coffee to volunteering a day to help someone move. Those are generous actions. Another example might be to say, 'I want to get along with people better,' but that is not very actionable either. But if you were to say, 'I would like to be a better communicator,' that is actionable. Resulting actions might include avoiding interrupting people, practicing being an active listener, and reflecting back what people say to you so that you're sure you understand what they're telling you."

"You want a list of traits that I feel I'm *lacking in* and want to improve, but they must be specific enough that I can translate that desire into decisions and actions."

"Yes, but it doesn't have to be areas that you're *lacking in* you could be good at them already and you just want to be better than you are now. There's always room for improvement in anything."

I nodded agreement. 'This is going to be a difficult list,' I thought.

Flying over West End

7

Incrementally

"It should be a lovely sunny morning, and the view of the island from the boat will be excellent," Paul remarked as the boat started to pull away from the Beach House dock in West End. We had hitched a lift aboard a charter boat called the *Ruthless* that was owned by some of Paul's friends. You could see that the history of the Roatan was steeped in pirates just by the choice of names on boats, bars and hotels on the island. The boat was going to be out for a few hours fishing, and then return to West End for breakfast. Paul had thought this trip would be a fun change from my daily diving routine, and as the boat surged out to sea through a path in the reef, I had to agree with him. This was the life!

Once the boat was a quarter of mile out from the dock, the captain turned to follow the coast towards West Bay and the crew threw out the fishing lines. We would be trawling back and forth; following the undersea drop-off in the hopes of catching a few large fish for the tourists on the boat. Looking forward as we approached West Bay, I could see the whole beach laid out before me in a long arcing white crescent edged by palm trees and hotels.

Following the fishing lines out with my eyes, I could see in the distance the lures bouncing on the surface of the sea and some dipping down and traveling below the surface of the water.

"Do you think they'll catch much?" I asked

"Sometimes they catch a lot, but sometimes there are dolphins in the water, and that scares the fish away. But I just like to sit up at the front of the boat and relax," replied Paul.

He motioned us forward along the side of the boat, and we took up position sitting near the bow.

"We're about to go round the end of the island," Paul pointed to the end of the beach, which looked even more picturesque than usual from this distance, as the white beach now blended into the green jungle-covered hills. From this distance, it looked flawless.

Noticing my stare, Paul said, "One day we'll mess it up, I'm sure. Build too many buildings. But for now, it looks almost untouched."

We stared back at the island as the boat moved slowly around the island's tip, and the coast changed from white beaches to the hard jagged iron shore.

With the sun still low in the sky, it wasn't too hot yet. We sat comfortably in silence for a while. Thinking back to my lessons from the day before, I relaxed, just absorbing the scene and also trying to be aware of the details. The slightly varying colors of the jungle. The splash of colors of the occasional building that popped up above the canopy. The different blues and greens that made up the colors of the sea, indicating different depths of water.

After a period of time, Paul turned to me and asked, "Ready to chat or would you rather just sit for a while?"

A little reluctantly, I pulled my attention away from the view and told him I was ready.

"Yesterday," said Paul, "we discussed what I believe are some of the foundations of taking control of your thoughts, your life and your happiness. We need to be able to still our inner voice so that it serves its purpose and no more. Otherwise, whenever a situation occurs that bothers us, we become slaves to its need to find answers. Meditation is the best way to do this that I have found so far. By allowing the mind to be still, by acknowledging thoughts but not being distracted by them, the voice diminishes and we become calmer.'

"It helps to set up a standard plan about who you are trying to be and how you would like to behave to others. That's why I use and teach the compassion exercise. It helps you let go of conflicts and issues that you're holding onto from your past. When you hold onto negative emotions, it's only you that is being hurt. So by actually practicing loving other people, we learn to forgive, and by forgiving, we free ourselves. In addition, it also helps improve your overall sense of wellbeing. You will find that you're slower to take offense, and quicker to be kind. Both of which contribute to your enjoyment of life. Then we looked at practicing mindfulness, or as I think of it, simply learning to enjoy and savor each moment. Finally, in the evening we talked about focus and how essential it is to direct your attention deliberately. By directing your attention, you're taking control of your thoughts and empowering yourself."

I indicated my agreement.

"I consider these all to be general conditioning exercises for your mind," he continued. "I believe they're useful in the extreme. If you only did these three exercises daily, you would see a radical transformation in your life. You would lead a happier and more fulfilled life without making any other changes. Though further changes would occur as a result of using them, of that I'm confident."

"Why don't you put it in a book?"

Paul looked around at me wistfully. "It's already in many books. People are impatient, they believe that someone out there has a secret formula to happiness. That once they learn the secret, it will change their whole personality and fix their life. It's just not going to happen that way. They devour self-help books, tossing one after another into the trash when it doesn't fix everything immediately. A lot, I agree, probably belong in the trash, but some offer practical advice. There just is no hidden secret to it. It takes time."

I felt a little bit of a guilty flush cross my face at the mention of self-help books. "But surely you can make changes quickly in your life," I said.

"Changes can seem to happen suddenly, but more often than not it's been a gradual build up. A person who has given up smoking for a long period has, in a sense, changed suddenly. One day he was smoking, the next day he was not. Further investigation might reveal that it's their seventeenth attempt that has finally stuck. Numerous attempts at change are a sign of a gradual building of desire or desperation to change.'

"Also, just because behavior has changed does not mean the underlying feelings and motivations have changed. It takes time to sink in new habits and mental conditioning. For instance, you might make immediate changes to your life because of an unexpected health scare. But it will take a long time to integrate those changes sufficiently into your life so that they're second nature, and you're truly transformed."

All this seemed disappointing to me. I thought quietly for a time, and Paul seemed content to let the conversation die while I reflected on what he had said.

After a while, the boat turned in a long arc and started another fishing pass. Paul quietly continued, "A good analogy is when you leave one job for another. Leaving a job may be a quick decision, it may be thrust upon you, or it could be a move made after long consideration. Once you start a new job, it of course requires different skills and methods than those you used in your previous job, some of which may be totally new to you. To be successful at this new job you need to learn, change, and then excel. You struggle to do the job at first. It can be difficult and stressful. Over time, you learn what you need, and then you master it. All the new skills become second nature to you. You can then move on to other roles with this new set of skills to excel in your chosen career.'

"No one when they first employ you truly believes you can take on a new role with all the skills necessary overnight. They know that any new position is going to be challenging and requires dedication to master. They also know that you're going to be doing it every day, and with time and coaching, you will learn and excel. They hire you because of your potential.'

"It's the same with changing yourself. It's not possible to be someone different overnight, it's possible to change some aspects of your behavior, and sometimes those changes may seem abrupt to others, but the real changes, the underlying conditioning, takes time. We do not realize how much we will change in the future. We always feel that we will be the same person. That this person we are today, the values we hold, our opinions, our temperament - all those aspects that we identify as ourselves - are somehow set."

"No, that's not true! I know I will be different in the years to come," I interjected.

"There is a substantial difference between an intellectual understanding of something and actually feeling it. I'm not picking on you, by the way," he apologized. "It's true for all of us. It has been shown again and again that people believe their core values hardly change over time. It's why we argue adamantly when anyone challenges our viewpoint. If we believed we were open to change, we would listen more and argue less.'

"This brings me to my fourth foundation: *Time will change us, so choose the change.* The undeniable fact is that we will not be the same person in the future, and how boring would it be if we were? We grow, we change. Our personality, values and even attitudes change. Once you grasp the fundamental fact that you will change, regardless of whether you want to change, then it's a small step to realize that you should take charge and direct that change. You cannot control your growth entirely, as your growth is a response to time passing and what life throws at you. But you can make choices about how you act in each moment, and about how you react in each moment. By making choices in a directed fashion, you can move yourself in the direction you desire to grow."

Paul paused again, and we both sat for awhile enjoying the slight fall and rise of the boat as it cut through the water. I agreed with what he was saying, but I felt that he hadn't said anything particularly helpful.

"This is all fascinating and I understand your perspective, but I feel like I need more details on how to create these changes. You haven't said anything specific, and just deciding to change doesn't make it happen. I might want to be one type of person, but looking back at my life, I don't think I've turned out the way I actually hoped."

I thought back to all the dreams I had for myself when I was at school. How it had all seemed so easy and straightforward. I would work my way up through a newspaper, become known for my insightful articles, and eventually become a world renowned journalist. Finally I would end up as an elder statesman of the news world. That had not been anything like reality. Bouncing from job to job as the newspaper market dissolved, churning out blog posts and superficial material as all news moved online and investigative reports seemed to be a thing of the past; this was my reality.

"Everyone has thoughts about who they want to be, Paul. But for me and many others, it hasn't worked out that way. Life intrudes on all our plans."

Paul noticed the slight bitterness that crept into my voice. "Fate is not totally the cause of who you are now," he replied. "Each of us in life will have challenges thrown at us, painful experiences to overcome, disasters to deal with. But on the flip side, we will have joys to savor and successes to enjoy. What differentiates each and every one of us are the choices we make to deal with each situation."

"So you think I should make the choice to be happy and optimistic? That just by making a choice I can change who I am."

"No," Paul said. "But yes as well," he added. "Let me explain," he put up his hand to prevent any interruption. "Yes, you do have to make the decision to be happy. That is and should be a bold and conscious choice on your part. Because without making that fundamental choice in your life, you won't do what is required. But choosing alone has no effect. None at all. Deciding to learn a musical instrument does not mean I can play one without practicing every day. The decision must come first, and it is meaningful only in that it leads to committed action. If you decide to do something and then follow through with study and practice, you will improve. You may never be a master, but you will improve. But just deciding has no effect. Only a decision followed by right action will get you closer to the results you desire."

"'Right action.' What do you mean by right action?"

"I stole that phrase from Buddhism," Paul acknowledged.

"I just liked it and it stuck with me. In Buddhism, it might mean generally to do no harm, or rather to take a Buddha-like action, which means not stealing, lying, cheating, harming others etc. I use it in a similar sense, in that you're doing the right thing at any point in time."

"Life is made up of choices. Sometimes these choices seem trivial, and sometimes they're impossibly hard. We tend to concentrate on the large choices in life as being the most important. Where to live, what to do? But what if I told you we had it wrong, that it's actually the small choices that are important? That it's the small choices we make that determine who we are in life? That making good small choices make big choices easier?"

"That seems a little ridiculous! So whether I choose to have sugar in my coffee is a more crucial choice than if I should accept a job offer?"

Paul said simply. "To a diabetic, putting sugar in coffee is an important choice."

"But I'm not a diabetic. It's not an important choice to me."

Paul held up his hand yielding the point. "Okay. Any one choice is not important in itself, I agree with you on that part, but my issue is once again that we do not take time into our equations. A rock cannot be harmed by a single rainfall, but raindrops falling year after year will eventually erode any rock into the path the water needs to escape. Do you think diabetics just wake up one day and choose to have the health problems they suffer from? No, unless the disease is the result of an underlying medical condition, it's often the result of years of small decisions. Those decisions most likely were not even noticeable at each point, but they do have consequences. Like your sugar and coffee example. Each decision is minor in itself, but the cumulative result over time can be emotionally and physically devastating."

It was my turn to hold my hand up to stave off interruption. "Even if I agree that what you're saying is true and that small decisions are important, did you not just tell me the other day that decisions take willpower and that we have a finite amount of willpower each day? So I need to avoid making a lot of decisions, because as soon as my willpower is depleted I will make poor ones. If I start monitoring all my decisions, I'll end up making lousy choices," I concluded.

I saw no flaw in my argument, and I watched Paul closely wondering how he would try to back out of one of his own arguments.

"I agree totally," he said.

I genuinely wished he wouldn't do that! Every time I felt I found a flaw in his arguments, he agreed with me. It was quite annoying. Like he was playing some kind of mental judo.

"Alright, I will stop trying to be so argumentative," I said, holding up my hands in mock-surrender. "If you can tell me how you can have it both ways at once. You want me to watch every small decision, but you tell me if I do I'll end up making poor decisions."

Paul nodded at my summary. "There is no way to avoid making decisions, but as always, we need to focus on how the brain works and work with it, not against it. What we need to do is try to condition the brain to respond one way, or to choose to do the right action without willpower. If we are clear on the outcome we desire and maintain a focus on that outcome throughout the day, then the mind will actually generate options for us. It will do so with little effort on our part."

"The best way to explain is to tell you about Benjamin Franklin."

"Benjamin Franklin as in the founding father and inventor?" I asked.

"Yes, the very same. He was a brilliant man, and decided early on in his life that if he wanted to succeed, both in business and society, he needed to hone certain traits. The traits he chose were common virtues of the time like hard work, sincerity and determination. Now, of course he would not be the first person in the world to think through which traits might be ideal for a successful life. We all do that. But Benjamin formulated a plan of action to cultivate these virtues. To develop them, if you like, so they became a core part of his personality.'

"What he did was simple in practice but profound in effect. He decided on thirteen virtues that he believed would enable him to succeed. He carefully envisioned how each virtue would manifest in his life. He defined it in detail. In essence, what he was doing was letting his mind know what behavior he was looking for with each virtue. Then, rather than trying to do all the virtues at once, which as we have discussed is a recipe for disaster, he focused on one virtue for a whole week. He would try to keep that virtue in his mind, so that it influenced his decisions moment by moment. As an example, imagine this week he was working on the virtue he called *Industry*, which was about remaining productive at all times. For that week he never let himself become idle or do something that was not productive in some way. By focusing his attention on only one virtue at a time, moment by moment, he soon fell into a pattern of looking at every situation through the lens of that virtue. The mind loves routine - routine conditions the mind to transform conscious decisions into unconscious behavior."

"But what about all the other virtues? Did he just let them slide while he was focusing on the one for that week?"

"No. That's the beauty of his system. By focusing on just one, he was conditioning his mind, and by the end of the week he was making better decisions in that area. When he moved onto the next virtue, his mind still retained the conditioning. Of course, his decisions based around the other twelve virtues were not as good as when he was a hundred percent focused on them, but the conditioning is there, the memory tracks laid, and there would be an incremental improvement. The more he practiced each virtue, the better he became at it. He would record his progress on each of his thirteen virtues on a scorecard every day, noting if he had slipped in any particular one.'

"A diary or log is another vital part of any attempt to change your behavior. You need to keep track. It doesn't matter what it is: eating, exercise, or changing habits; you need to have a way of constantly reviewing how well you're doing. It helps you create feedback loops that keep you moving in the direction that you desire to go."

"How long did he keep this up for?" I asked, suspecting I knew the answer.

Paul tilted his head and gave me a quizzical look.

I sighed. "Forever, right? Because, as you say, we never stop growing or changing."

Paul nodded. "Yes, all his life. You change regardless, over time, so choose to make the changes you want in your life. You don't have to follow in Benjamin's footsteps, though they're good ones to follow. You don't need to pick broad virtues as he did, but for a long term plan I see his choices as being excellent ones."

"Which virtues did actually choose?" I asked.

"I think I can list them," Paul said, creasing his forehead a little in thought. "He divided them up into two groups. Personal traits that he believed would help him achieve his business and life goals, and social traits that be believed would help him in his dealings with others."

"The social traits are," Paul held up his hand in front of him and counted them off on his fingers, "*Temperance, Silence, Order, Resolution, Frugality, Moderation, Industry and Cleanliness.* That's eight, and then the five personal traits are *Sincerity, Justice, Tranquility, and Chastity.*" Paul stopped counting, though he was one short of five.

"There is a story that he originally only came up with twelve traits; when he revealed his plans to his colleagues, a close friend came to him and told him that he had missed one. His friend pointed out that he was often arrogant and talked down to people. After a little persuading and some pointed examples, he added the last one, *Humility.*"

Paul chuckled to himself. "It's good to have friends. They keep you grounded."

"Well, at least I know why you wanted me to come up with those behaviors yesterday."

"What did you come up with?" asked Paul.

After hearing Franklin's list, I was a bit ashamed of mine. But I told him anyway. "Politeness, Focus, Drive, Generosity and Forgiveness"

"What do you mean by politeness?" asked Paul, looking

puzzled.

I look slightly guilty. "Well, I had it drawn to my attention a little while ago that I'm somewhat addicted to my smartphone. I tend to carry it everywhere and often rudely gravitate toward it in the presence of company. But there are also other points; I think I have become a little too quick to forget the personal touch. Not enough time spent with real people and too much time in front of my computer. So I feel I need to keep my phone at home sometimes, or at least in my pocket. To spend quality time with family and friends rather than being there physically while my mind is elsewhere."

Paul nodded, "I have suffered from that particular addiction too. Sadly, I think it is a common addiction. I'm glad you brought up the bit about spending quality time with your family and friends - that's an indication that you view them as valuable, and it's good to hear. Study after study show they're vital to your long-term happiness and health. Having a good social support structure can add many potential years to your life."

"How do I actually put this list into action?" I asked.

"To use your list, you just need to spend some time going through each trait, understanding what it means to you and what it is you're trying to improve. It's fine if you wish to focus on just one bad habit, but maybe your desired focus is much wider. For instance, politeness may just mean paying attention to people while you're physically with them, but it may have many other implications. What is it that you're actually trying to achieve? To connect with people more, or to be more respectful or both? Or something else entirely? If it is to be more respectful to others, then maybe you should add in details of how you wish to interact with them; listening and asking questions. If it is to connect with people more, maybe you should start planning meetings with others at coffee shops or in your home."

"Once you understand what it is that you're actually trying to achieve, expand your definition so that it will guide you when you have choices to make. For instance, if you were trying to connect more with people, you might accept an invitation to spend time with people that you would usually refuse. When you run into people by accident, you may ask them to coffee. When you're introduced to someone new, you might try to show more interest in them than you would do otherwise. By focusing on the behavior you will make your choices reflect your desired goals, but eventually those choices will become natural and subconscious.'

"After you know what you want, set yourself a regular schedule of up to a week. You could even do one a day, but I think longer is better. But focus on trying to make a decision in line with what you're trying to achieve. Once again, we're back to the concept that you're consciously choosing to direct and focus your mind to guide it along paths you want it to develop. You are conditioning your mind so that it will begin to make choices instinctively and subconsciously that reflect those values that you wish to have in your life.'

"Remember, you're going to grow, and you're going to change. The only difference between someone who practices these techniques and someone who does not is that the practitioners have decided not to leave the direction of their growth up to fate; they have taken their destiny in their own hands and chosen the path their life is going to take."

"I call this conscious growth. You are choosing to grow as a person. To shed those characteristics you don't like and embrace those that you wish to embody. A conscious decision to grow is empowering. You are no longer a victim of circumstances. No matter what the world throws at you, you are the architect of your life. Because life is not just a series of events, good or bad. It's the path that leads between and through those events. So choose the direction you wish to take."

Paul paused. I hadn't realized how intense and serious he had grown with those last words. He moved his eyes back toward the line of beaches on the horizon

"I think we both have had enough of my lecturing for this morning. Let's go back and join the others and see if we can catch some fish for lunch."

He pushed himself up using the rail for support as the boat moved slowly up and down. Looking back at me, his face took on an impish look.

"Are you doing much after you to return to the hotel?" he asked.

"No, nothing planned. Why?"

"Oh I have a vital errand to run and thought you might like to come along. I'll pick you up later," and with that he started making his way to the back of the boat.

West End Sunset

8

Field Trip

Paul picked me up from the entrance of the Henry Morgan after lunch. As soon as I jumped into his car, I was thankful again for the invention of air conditioning. The heat wasn't too oppressive, but after spending the morning in the sun on the boat, I was grateful for some time spent in a cool environment.

"Where are we off to now?" I asked Paul as he negotiated the exit from the hotel and turned away from West Bay.

Not taking his eyes from the road, Paul accelerated up the steep hill out of West Bay. I had asked him earlier why he had such a large car for such a small island. Power, he had said while pointing to the hills surrounding the beach. Now, driving up the hill, I knew what he meant; a smaller car might not have made it up.

"We're going on a field trip to see the work of the world's leading experts in behavioral economics."

That sounded interesting. I wondered if we were visiting a university or a medical clinic of some kind. I had heard of neither being located on the island. As we drove, Paul pointed out a myriad of sights on the way. The majority of the island seemed to be covered in abundant green jungle. Paul explained that many of the island's residents lived in those areas, and it was just the dense covering of undergrowth along the road that hid them. From the air, it would look noticeably different. A few minutes out from West Bay, we found ourselves on a long road that hugged the water's edge.

The road was so windy that Paul was forced to travel extremely slowly. Both sides of the road were lined with wood houses, many of which were in disrepair.

At the entrance to Coxen Hole, Paul pointed out a large concrete pier that projected out from the road into the sea. It was surrounded by a high wall, and the dock was covered in buildings. This is one of the parts of Roatan that also serves as a cruise ship dock.

"There are often two cruise ships docked at once here," said Paul. "They can bring as many as 5,000 passengers per ship, though not all of them get off to see the island. You can always tell on the beach when there is a ship docked because of the massive influx of tourists, but the passengers have to leave by 3 PM, so the beach is once again deserted."

Paul wound his way through the town of Coxen Hole, finally coming out onto Roatan's only main road. Within seconds, he had turned off the main road and was pulling up a hill towards a large building.

"We're here," he announced. I looked carefully at the building; there was no mistaking what it was. I turned to him incredulously.

"It's a supermarket," I said simply.

"Yep!" He said, enjoying my look and exiting the car.

As I exited, he called across the roof, "I need some groceries, and you need to understand how easily we are all manipulated, and there are no more qualified manipulators than the people who try to convince us to buy their stuff."

He led the way through the doors and grabbed a shopping cart. He leaned on the back of the cart and swept his arm in an arc to include the entire store in the discussion.

"This store has been engineered down to the last detail to entice you, manipulate you, and just downright deceive you. Marketers know more about our behavior than we do. They spend a lot of money researching human behavior, with the clear goal of selling you products. What's more, it doesn't matter that you might be aware you're being manipulated, because most of what they do exploits biases we're not aware of at a conscious level."

"Do you know the majority of us have a right side bias? We are guided to the right as we enter the store because we prefer to look left for our groceries."

I shook my head.

"They do!" He said and pushed his cart to the right. The fresh fruit and vegetable section came into view as we neared the corner of the store.

"Fresh flowers, fruit and vegetables are always at the beginning of your shopping tour. Which makes no sense, as they're the most likely to get damaged when you put all the rest of your shopping items on top of them. But the marketers don't care, because they know that if we buy fruit and vegetables first, we feel like we are being healthy and then are more likely to buy processed food later."

Pointing to the mirrored cases holding the vegetables, he continued, "Even the presentation is there to give you the illusion of freshness. They spray water on the produce to give it a fresh look. It's not about keeping them fresh. In reality, some of the products have taken months to get to the store."

Throwing some food into the cart, he continued to the back of the store. He moved quickly down the back aisle. "You will generally find items that people buy regularly like milk, juice, etc. at the back of the store," he called backwards over his shoulder, "so that you have to travel through the store to get to them. Which of course means you will be tempted by other items on the way."

He stopped in front of one item that was priced at 99 Lempira. "Why do you think they price like that?" Indicating the label.

"Because it feels a lot lower than 100," I answered.

"Yes," he said "simply because it works. It doesn't matter that you know the price is artificially fixed at that point. You can even reason that the price has been manipulated to 'feel' lower. It still works. If it didn't work, they would stop doing it. Profits are all they care about."

He pointed back down the central aisle at a long rack of wine. "Do you notice the music?" he asked.

Up to that point I hadn't been aware of any. "Not really." I said.

"They research everything. Slower music, you move through the store slowly. Play French music in the wine aisle and people will tend to buy more French wine. Play German music and more German wine will be purchased."

He left the cart where it was and moved over to the wine, and I followed along. "Look at these wines." He pointed to a small section of wines. "Let me convert these to dollars for you. This one is about $5, that one's $7, that one's $12, and that one's $25. How many people take the $25 a bottle, do you think?"

"Not many," I answered.

"What if I told you the expert manipulators truly don't care? That the bottle is only there to anchor the price higher for all the other wines. You see, you're influenced by the price of that bottle even if you would never consider buying it. The expensive bottle establishes a larger price range in your mind, pulling your choice towards the $12 bottle. You may tell others you choose your wine based on taste alone, but the marketers know the truth. Most people just buy from the higher end of the range, but rarely the most expensive. Even if someone produced an award winning wine and it was the cheapest on the aisle, many people wouldn't buy it."

He turned around to the other side, which was filled with chips and snacks.

"If you look at the shelves," he said, "all the products they want you to buy will be at eye level. When they're selling to children, the products will be at the eye level of a child."

He moved on, "Come on, let's keep moving."

"Why are we hurrying?" I asked, trailing behind him.

He called out over his shoulder. "It's my way to fight back and keep impulse purchases to a minimum. Never shop hungry! Move quickly and always know what you need to buy. They fight back, of course. Have you ever walked into your supermarket and noticed that they have moved everything around so you can't find what you're looking for any more? They do it for that exact reason. They don't like you to know where the food you want is located;

they want you to have to browse to find it. That way, you may discover and buy other items."

Grabbing his cart, he continued down towards the back of the store. I moved quickly to keep up with him. As we neared the other end of the aisle, a lovely aroma of freshly baked bread greeted us. Paul moved down the aisle and picked items quickly and with a practiced ease. He did indeed, seem to know what he was looking for in each aisle. He stopped and turned, showing me a product label.

"They spend a lot of time finding the words that grab you. Words like natural, fat free, healthy to name a few. When there is a current fad for a certain additive like Omega 3, you can be sure that remarkably quickly it will be displayed prominently on the labels. Look at this one," he pointed to a particular item. "Have you ever thought that 95% fat free is the same as 5% fat? Do you think they would sell as much food labeled with 10% fat rather than 90% fat free?" He said wistfully, "I think not!"

Putting the item back on the shelf, he continued. "What is necessary to understand is that these companies spend a lot of money learning the best way to influence you. From the packaging, the branding, the words, everything is checked and rechecked. They always follow the money. If an item survives on the shelves, or a method of selling continues to be used, it's because it works. Come on, let's get out of here and grab a coffee."

He made his way to the checkout and loaded his few items in front of the clerk. "And of course they keep the most tempting items till you're stuck standing at the checkout." He said, holding up chocolate from a large selection in front of him. He let it fall back into the display.

Once we were outside, he stuck his meager collection of supplies into the back of his vehicle, and we climbed back into his car. The cafe was only a short drive away, in front of another supermarket.

From the cafe, you could see all over Coxen Hole and toward the cruise ship dock. The town was a complicated assortment of rundown old buildings and brightly-colored newer ones. Often, the old and the new stood side by side. I sat down at a small round table, and Paul ordered some drinks from the counter and joined me.

"Alright," he said sitting back and looking a lot more relaxed. "Sorry for the rush, but there was a real purpose behind taking you to the supermarket. We have discussed many things: how to formulate habits, how to condition your mind to still your inner voice and generally how to improve your choices. These are yours to take control of, it just takes time and conviction."

"Now, I want you to think about those things you can't control. Those areas in life where you need your inner voice to override your normal feelings and emotion. We like to think of ourselves as rational creatures making decisions thoughtfully, or at least fairly. The idea that we are rational beings has been part of our culture for a long time. Our entire economic system was built upon the belief that people think things through and make rational decisions about what is best for them. The truth is, we don't; we are irrational beings. Once you admit that, then you can be on guard against it. If you cannot admit that to yourself, then you will be manipulated constantly."

The coffee had arrived on the table. Paul paused to add a little milk to his coffee. I took the opportunity to clarify something.

"If it has been believed for so long that we are rational creatures, how is it that you believe we are not?"

"In the last few decades, we have begun to better understand how the brain works, and in the last few years, the pace of that understanding has accelerated. Scientists can actually study areas of the brain in real time as they're being used with the use of advance scanners. Human beings evolved to survive in a world remarkably different from the one we live in now. In that world, like most animals, we were ruled by few basic tenets. Essentially: eat, avoid danger, have sex, conserve energy. Not necessarily in that order."

I laughed.

"Yes! We were, and still are that basic," he pointed out. "Anyway, our extraordinary brain is actually broken into multiple parts. It's not a single functioning organism directed by an overlord. It's more like a team of specialists, each one putting forward their point of view with our friend the narrator thrown into give us some clarity and identity."

"I like that analogy better than a room full of middle level managers," I said.

"I agree it sounds more elegant that way. The brain has developed shortcuts to evaluate information quickly and give you a speedy answer. You see, in the wild, you may not have time to sit and ponder every decision. Your life may be on the line, and you have to react fast. Even when you have the time to sit and think, your brain uses far more energy doing so. Thinking consciously takes time and energy, both precious commodities when you're trying to survive. Let me give you an example. When someone unexpectedly taps you on the shoulder, or you suddenly feel something brush against your leg, you jump quickly. You do not stop, turn around, evaluate the danger and decide what to do. You just jump. How high depends more on your emotional state than anything else. If you were frightened or tense, your reaction would be stronger. If you were walking in a dangerous place after dark, you might even scream as you jump. The fact that you were already on the alert for danger makes it more likely you will react strongly. It's fascinating that the brain can't tell the difference between fake fear and real fear. If you watch a horror movie, you might have exactly the same reaction as if you were terrified by a real life situation. Your brain would be pumping chemicals into your body while you watched the movie, making sure it's ready to react. On the other hand, if you were relaxed because you had just had a nap or a pleasant massage, you wouldn't be primed to be scared. You might still jump, but not in the same manner."

Pausing to take a sip from his coffee, he continued. "So we all recoil from the unknown, especially when we're scared. Nothing strange about that, but my point is that you don't think about it. So how does it happen and happen so fast? Essentially, your physical reaction has an extremely direct route that bypasses any higher mental functions. As you're flying away from the stimulus your mind has time to catch up with events, and you can finally evaluate the threat."

"In a similar way, the brain has evolved other less primitive shortcuts to make quick decisions on scant information. Catching a ball is a formidable example. The brain takes in a tremendous amount of information from the eye and uses it to guide a hand into the exact position to catch the ball and absorb the impact. It's an extremely impressive feat that takes little conscious attention. There are more subtle shortcuts, as when the brain uses perspective and the height of objects to judge distances. These shortcuts are the basis of many optical illusions."

He stopped and took a folded piece of paper from his pocket. "I printed these out earlier today so you could see them," he said.

"The first one shows how our mind likes to complete concepts from incomplete information. It makes a triangle where none exists."

I looked over the paper. I had seen these and many like them before. I found them interesting and a lot of fun, but I was not entirely sure where he was heading.

"The second one epitomizes how our mind can only focus on one concept at a time. As your eye moves around the points of the triangle, it changes form. Similarly, you cannot be focused on the good aspects and the bad aspects of a situation at the same time.

Reviewing the second image, I added. "So we have parts of the brain that automate key tasks. That makes sense; if it speeds up our thought processes, it's beneficial."

"Before you put that paper away, realize one critical point Even though you know it's an illusion, you can't stop seeing the illusion. You cannot tell your mind that it's not real and get your brain to stope generating the illusion. You can only say to yourself 'I know what I'm seeing is not real!' You see the illusion still, but you can take a mental step sideways, knowing what you're seeing is incorrect and taking action accordingly."

"Yes, I see that," I agreed.

"Well, we have lots of shortcuts in the brain about how we judge situations, and scientists are discovering more all the time. There are literally hundreds of them. You can't stop them even if you're aware of them. Aware or not, they influence your perception of reality. As some people like to say, *perception is reality*, so it helps to know about those shortcuts so that you can defend against them."

I folded the paper and gave it back to him. He dropped it on the plate in front of him, no longer seeming to care for it now that its message was given.

"I'm sure at this point everything I'm saying is somewhat academic, and you're wondering how it relates to what we have been discussing in our talks - especially in the context of happiness."

"A little, yes. So far, you have been helping me condition my mind for happiness and do exercises that will direct my life the way I want it to go. I'm not sure how I can use this information. Especially if, as you say, I can't stop my mind from functioning this way."

Paul sat considering my question for a moment. "I think the best way is to show you." He pushed his drink to the center of the table and stood up. "Let's go!"

We were quickly back in his car and moving towards West End. "Sometimes a demonstration is far better than an explanation," he said as he drove.

Fifteen minutes later, we passed West End and turned towards West Bay. After a few turns of the road, Paul pulled over to the side of the road by a large wooden building.

"This is a bar and restaurant called Roatan Oasis, owned by some friends of mine. They won't mind me kidnapping one of their TVs for a minute. I want to show you something that I can't show you at my house since I don't have a TV."

"Really?" I said, unbelievably.

"Haven't had one for years," he added as he walked up a short set of the stairs into the building. He turned left at the top of the stairs into a modern and warmly decorated bar.

"Hi Paul!" came a welcoming shout from behind the bar.

"Never been here before," he joked. "Can I borrow your TV for a moment? I want to show my friend something," Paul shouted back.

"Sure, no problem. Just turn it off when you're done with it."

Paul led me over to a sectional couch. On the opposing wall was a large screen TV. Paul walked over to it and picked up the remote that was resting on the top of the screen. Using the remote, he quickly switched through the channels until he hit a 24 hour news channel. He adjusted the volume on the TV so it was loud enough to hear clearly.

"Just watch for few minutes," said Paul.

It was a typical news channel with about a 15-minute cycle for news. We must have been about halfway through the cycle when Paul finally muted it in disgust.

"Have you ever watched one of these channels for a long time? Maybe when there was a crisis or some kind of significant news event on?" he asked.

"Yes," I admitted. "I have."

"It's curious to me how we need to feel constantly up-to-date when there is some kind of breaking news event. It's like we are somehow involved or there is something we can actually do about it. There is a strange need for immediacy and intimacy with current events. A need for us to be aware of information in real time, whereas in actuality we could read a summary of the week's events and be better informed in a fraction of the time."

"I suppose that's true," I said, glancing at the TV. The highlights of a football game were now being shown. "But it's important sometimes to be in sync with everyone else. If you're watching a sports game on TV, you have no effect on that game, but it's more fun to watch it live and cheer along."

"Yes. A sports game is necessary to watch live because the pleasure of sports is in how the game unfolds. Also, it's often a social event with lots of emotion invested in the sport and the teams you follow. The news, however, is not usually enjoyable; in fact, most people find it depressing, especially in the way it's packaged currently by the media."

Paul put down the TV remote by his side and made himself comfortable on the couch facing the TV. "Let me explain what this has to do with our field trip to the supermarket, and why I believe watching the news in this manner is incredibly bad for your state of mind."

Intrigued, I sat down on the opposite end of the couch facing Paul and motioned for him to continue.

"I mentioned earlier that the mind has evolved many shortcuts to streamline the thinking process. These shortcuts, or cognitive biases as they're correctly called, have evolved for a reason, and they work extremely well. Unfortunately, the environment that they developed in doesn't exist anymore. Actions we had to take trying to survive hunting on the plains make little sense in the modern world."

I was still having trouble pulling together everything Paul was telling me. "What do you mean by these cognitive biases?"

"Well, it's the nature of these biases that we are blind to them and can often only clearly see the effects when they're studied. It's usually easier to see them in others than in ourselves. The best way to explain is to list some of these biases, and show you how your perception of reality is warped by them."

"The reason I'm showing you the news is that it feeds into one of the most common and disturbing biases we have. The availability bias is a shortcut to judging the probability of a future event. The easier we can recall an event happening in the past, the more likely we are to believe it will happen in the future. This bias exists because we humans are not instinctively good at math or probability. We have no feel for large numbers, and our ability to grasp how likely something is to happen is frankly pathetic. We combine dissimilar events into simple groupings like *unlikely*, *certain* and *likely*. In reality, events that are wildly improbable are lumped together with events that are almost certain. An obvious demonstration of that is the lottery. On a recent mega lottery, the odds were so ridiculously high against winning that you had more chance of correctly picking a random day in the future when an individual was going to be hit by lightning than of winning. If I asked you to bet your hard-earned money on predicting lightning hitting someone, you would think I was insane and would never take the bet. Yet people play the lottery constantly."

Idly pointing his finger to the ceiling, Paul continued. "If I look at the sky and I see a few clouds on the horizon, how likely is it to rain?" He pointed down, "If I hear rustling from the undergrowth, how likely is it to be a snake or a tiger? How does our mind figure out how likely something is to happen?"

"We have developed a simple system to figure out its likelihood. The brain just says to itself, 'How easy is it to recall this happening before?' Literally the easier it is to remember an event, the more strongly you feel that it's going to happen again. We remember seeing lottery winners happy and excited on the news, and so it feels likely. If the news read out the names of the millions of people who did not win, not only would it take years to do on TV, you would never play the lottery because your brain would finally get the concept."

"Notice I said *feel* how likely it is to happen because to us probability is a feeling. It's not mathematics. It feels likely, it feels unlikely. We feel it," he touched his stomach, "that's why we call it a 'gut feeling' when we think something is going to happen."

"So the clouds in the sky mean rain, if we remember rain recently. The rustling on the ground makes us terrified if we saw a snake earlier or the fear of them is present in our mind. You might say that's sensible on both counts, and that's my point. The brain uses its ease of recall as a quick way to determine how we feel about a future event simply because it works!'

"Or rather, it did work until we became civilized. The inner certainty we feel about an event happening is independent of the real possibility of it happening. It's just related to how well we can remember something similar. There may not exist any chance of a storm. There may be no snakes in that part of the country. Our brain doesn't care. If we can recall it, then it's a possibility. The easier it is to remember, the more likely it *feels* it's going to happen."

Paul paused and picked up the remote and pointed it at the TV. "What has this to do with the TV and our state of mind? Well, what do you see when you look at the news in this form? Endless repetition of horrific events. Often the same event mindlessly repeated. Most likely the events shown are nowhere near you, they don't affect you and have an exceedingly small chance of ever affecting you. Even if the news did intersect your life in some way, the amount of repetition is in no way related to its actual relevance to your life. What this does," gesturing at the TV again with the remote, "is generate unreasonable fear in people, and distorts their perception of reality."

"Are you suggesting people just bury their heads in the sand and forget about the world? We can't all live on an island in an ignorant-but-happy bubble!"

"No, not at all! It's necessary to be informed and to take part, where possible, in what is going on in the world. I'm suggesting that you already live in a bubble by watching this medium, but not a bubble of your choosing. You are fed horror, violence and disturbing news continuously because it keeps people hooked. If the news media actually showed you matters that most people should be concerned about in their daily lives, the news would be very different. TV shows would be informative and probably boring to watch. The format of news distorts our view of the world by reporting the emotionally-charged events *ad nauseum* and without a sense of proportion simply because that's what gets your attention. "

"Well, what should the news be showing us then?"

"Not this!" He turned off the TV in disgust. "It plays straight into the bias I mentioned earlier. We can easily recall all this horror, and why not? We see it all the time. Our mind now thinks these events are likely in our own lives, when they're not. We bring the fear of these exceptional events into our daily lives. I'm not denying the existence of terrible things happening in the world, just that our sense of perspective is totally missing. People live in fear where no reasonable fear need exist."

"I talk to people who worry so much about dying at the hands of a stranger, or in a plane crash, or by shark attack, when the realities of this situation are that for almost everyone in the first world, it's not going to happen. Fear dominates our cultures, and we spend vast amounts of time and resources worrying about unlikely events. Instead, we should concentrate on events that can actually make a difference in our lives and those of people around us. Concentrating on health and nutrition alone would make a significant difference to our lifespan. The act of practicing compassion and helping others, rather than fearing them, would allow us to live longer and happier lives."

"That is not reality," he said, indicating the TV. "That is a fear bubble, and you need to find a better way to get the information that you need to know about and act upon."

He sat back down on the couch, staring at the now black screen. "I often tell people vacationing here that the most dangerous part of the trip was the drive to and from the airport - most do not believe me. They remember horrifying plane crashes on the news and so they fear flight. It's far safer to be traveling by plane than by car. Sometimes I find people hanging back from the water down at the beach, and I find out that they're terrified of sharks in the water. I explain that there has never been a shark attack here, and that sharks are rare. I even point out that, statistically, they're far more likely to die from a coconut falling on their head than a shark attack."

"Did that help?" I asked.

"No. I think I just made them afraid of coconut trees," he sighed sadly.

"Isn't our fears of sharks just a natural and instinctive fear of a large dangerous predator?" I said.

"No, it's not. Before the movie in the 70s called *Jaws*, people were not that afraid of sharks when they entered the water because they had no thought of sharks or the possibility of a shark attack in their minds. Now, after all the TV shark attack specials, it's embedded within our cultural psyche. A perfect example of what I'm trying to explain. We have invented a fear because our brain can recall it easily. An average of ten people a year, in the entire world, die of shark attacks, and the attacks usually occur in certain well-known spots. Compare that to the nearly half million people that die from drowning and boat accidents. Sharks may be a silly example, but if you compared deaths caused by terrorism or criminals versus deaths caused by diabetes, you would get a similar kind of ratio. The media concentrates on subjects that we cannot affect on a daily basis, such as frightening and spectacular news in faraway places, to the detriment of subjects like health and local community that significantly and directly affect their watchers and that their watchers can do something about."

We grew quiet for a while as I thought over what he had been saying. The news, to me, was sensationalistic and fear mongering, but I had never thought that it might be affecting my decisions.

"You mentioned other biases?" I asked.

"Yes. That's only one of many biases that affect us on a daily basis. There's one they call the *confirmation bias*, and it's particularly insidious in today's polarized society. This particular shortcut prevents us from being open-minded. It probably evolved so that we stopped second-guessing our tribe's ruling and acted as a single social unit. Confirmation bias affects the way we look at new information on a particular subject. Once we form an opinion, we lose our impartiality. We subconsciously believe any information that confirms our current thinking, and dismiss information that argues against it. We still believe we are unbiased and rational creatures, but we're not. Presented with two different arguments based on the same data, we would believe the one that confirmed our current thinking. This has been tested time and time again. We are never impartial once we have subconsciously made up our mind. The result is that people think they're open minded, but they're not."

"Well, if you're unaware of your lack of impartiality, how can you guard against it?" I asked.

Looking grim, Paul said, "There you have the crux of the matter. First, most people aren't aware there even is such a bias, so how can they guard against it? They think they're being fair, but their mind is already filtering the information. Second, even if you're aware of it, it's a subconscious process, and it's extraordinarily difficult to be impartial. All you can do is be aware that you might have emotionally made up your mind one way and that you're probably not giving the other point of view a fair consideration. The best we can hope for is to be reasonable to another person's position."

"This leads smoothly into another bias. We have a tendency to see our thoughts and beliefs as unbiased and other peoples' as being far from impartial. It's like a blind spot that makes us able to see others' flaws and motivations but blinds us to our own. You see, we tend to create our own 'bubbles,' to use your word, and most of the time we're unaware we live inside these bubbles. We seek out people with similar views, we seek out confirming facts for our viewpoints, we believe that others think the same way as we do when they rarely do. We do this all naturally and without forethought.'

"If you want to combat this, you need to force yourself to seek out people who disagree with you, seek out information that conflicts with your beliefs, and learn to listen to those that disagree with you. Now, this is unnatural for us and can be difficult and stressful. It's uncomfortable to be around people who disagree with us. When we are infuriated by someone else's viewpoint, it's natural to avoid them. We do this daily and subconsciously on a small scale in our social interactions. We select who we spend time with so that our daily lives are more comfortable."

"Trying to keep an open mind is something we all believe we do but actually, we close our mind every day in small ways. Keeping it open takes daily effort and lots of compassion. Another reason compassion meditation is so valuable."

His eyebrows raised questioningly. "You're going to keep doing the meditations?"

I nodded yes, "I've made a commitment to myself to do it every day for a month."

"Just remember, time is your friend. Miss one day on a particular task and that is no matter. Just do it the next day, as long as you always return to it. Over time, you will reap the benefits of any change you want to make in your life."

Paul got up and made as if to leave, and then sat down. "One more point, and it's a crucial one. If I could make everyone in the world understand and accept this one point, I swear we would have fewer wars, and society as a whole would be a better place to live in."

"Another of your small claims?"

Paul looked a little abashed. "Yes, I do get a little carried away sometimes, I apologize, but I will stand by the claim and let you be the judge."

"You see, when we meet others who have a different viewpoint from us, at first we just think they don't understand the issue. Obviously, they don't have all the facts about the issue or they would agree with you. When you discuss matters, and you find that they do indeed know their facts, you feel they must be stupid. If you realize that they're not stupid, that they know the same facts you do, then the conclusion is that they're malevolent in some way. In reality, they just have a different value set than you. They value certain aspects of an issue differently than you do. If you talk to them and try to understand their values, you will go a long way to understanding people who differ from you."

"This is hardly earth shattering, Paul. I think a lot of people understand that good people can hold different views and that those views are the product of their differing values. I think I'm going to have to say you failed in your outrageous claim."

"Ah, be patient. I haven't started, I was just getting in the mood. I think I'll tell you something that happened to me the other week to explain my point."

"I love to play poker. Poker is about understanding people and probability. I find the whole process of watching people as enthralling as the game itself. There are people at my poker club who are better than me, but I count myself as one of the better players."

"Is that a cognitive bias too?" I joked.

Paul laughed so hard I thought he was going to hurt himself. As he quieted down he stammered out, "Th-that was too funny and perfect! Perfect because there is indeed a bias where we overestimate our ability compared to others. We overestimate it when we think we are good at something and underestimate when we think we are inept at something. A perfect example is the way most people believe they're above average drivers, which isn't possible—mathematically, half the drivers in the world have to be below average."

"It's good to see that you can laugh at yourself while making such claims," I said.

Calmer now, Paul said with mock severity, "If you will let me finish before making any other jokes."

"Pray continue," I said, matching his tone.

"All right, while I was playing my usual brilliant game," he stared at me as if inviting comment. When none came, he continued. "I was dealt pretty good hole cards of an Ace and Queen of the same suit. After a round or two of betting, there were a few of us left in the round, and when the flop showed up, I was greeted with 3 cards matching my suit. I had flopped the best hand possible. I'm sorry, do you understand poker?" he interrupted himself.

"Well, not really, but I get the concept."

"Okay. It's sufficient to say that because my cards were all the same suit, I had a flush - often a winning hand. I had the ace of that suit in my hand, which is the top card, so I knew at that point I was almost a sure winner. By this time, all of the cards were finally on the table. I knew without a doubt that no other hand could possibly beat mine, and I put all my remaining money into the pot.

I had to remain calm as I wanted the other player to think I was bluffing with bad cards so they would add their money to the pot. But inside, I was so excited and supremely confident of winning. Without any hesitation, one of the other players put all his money into the pot. We both quickly turned over our cards, I saw that he had a lower flush than mine, and I reached forward to claim my money, only to be stopped by the hand of my opponent.

'Mine, I think,' he smirked. I looked down at our cards and saw with a sick feeling that I had misread my cards. That my cards were the same color, but not the same suit. Rather than having the best hand on the table, I had the worst possible. I was pretty much laughed off the table by the other players for my mistake."

Paul paused in thought. I could see it was an awkward memory, but hardly earth-shattering.

Thinking about his predicament, I inquired, "Your point is that if you act on incorrect information you can make a terrible mistake, and that you always need to double check your information before making big decisions like betting all your money?"

Paul shook his head as if to clear his mind. "No, not at all. Though, that is indeed a good point."

"Then what is your point?" I asked.

"Well, what do you think it felt like to me, to be wrong?"

"Awful, I guess. No one likes to be laughed at, especially when their mistake is plain to see and cannot be denied."

"No." Paul said calmly but forcefully, "You didn't answer the question I asked."

"What did it feel like? Yes, I did."

"No. You just told me what it felt like to discover I was wrong. Which, as you said, was awful. I was asking what it felt like to be wrong. Before I discovered my mistake."

"Well you said you felt great, excited and supremely confident."

Suddenly it hit me, and I grasped what he meant. It was quite a sickening thought.

Paul could see I got it. "You understand now?"

"Yes." Yes, I did.

"So what does it feel like to be wrong?" He asked again.

"It feels like you're right." I answered.

"Yes, you understand. Your feeling of certainty in the correctness of the truth, of righteousness in your cause, has no connection at all with the facts or the truth of your argument. It merely reflects your state of mind. Every time you find out you have been wrong about something, there will have been a period where you were certain you were right. Try to remember that next time you're sure you're in the right."

French Angelfish

9

Fundamentals

The editor was pleased with my work. I had managed to stretch the original article into the entire series my editor had hoped for, justifying the cost of sending me here. Not enough, though, to extend my trip as I had requested. He was pressing me to wrap it up and dig up more background details on Paul. As I gathered my notes together on the table, I admitted to myself that I was insanely curious about him too. Paul had a way of deflecting questions, even pointed ones, about his past, and the answers I did receive were rarely helpful. Yet, he was totally open about himself and his life in the present. The smallest question would send him off telling amusing anecdotes about his life here. It just seemed as if his life had begun here on Roatan. Searches of his background had been entirely fruitless. I had even begun to suspect that he was using a false name, as rarely do you draw a complete blank on someone.

I knew I shouldn't dive that day, as it was my last day prior to flying home - a necessary precaution to avoid the bends when flying in pressurized planes. The inconvenience of missing the last day's diving was nothing compared to the possibility of that painful condition. So I had spent the day alternating between the heat of the beach and poring over my notes of my stay in my air conditioned hotel room.

I looked at my phone to check the time. It was 4 PM. Today was our last meeting. I still had so many questions for him. Too many to ask in one day, never mind one meeting. I had to focus today. I had learned so much from him, but I needed information about him and his background to give my articles more impact. Who was Paul Halentine, and how had he become the person he is now?

Paul had arranged a driver to pick me up and take me to the Mayoka Lodge, a boutique hotel in Sandy Bay. He had been spending the day with some friends there and wanted me to come over and join him for dinner and enjoy my last sunset on the island. Sandy Bay was only ten minutes away, and soon I was being driven through a set of high gates that marked the grounds of the Lodge.

I took the time to take in my surroundings as I arrived. The Mayoka Lodge was situated on an acre of land. The main house had several large octagonal rooms at the back, clustered around an infinity-edged pool looking out over an extensive sandy beach. The sand was a light brown color, different from the white sands of West Bay where I had been staying. This beach was strung with many long wooden docks that jutted way out into the water. The shallow water, filled with turtle grass and edged by the occasional mangrove tree, hardly moved except for the passing of the occasional water taxi. Far out, the sea was marked by white foam as the outer reef broke the usual waves of the sea and enforced calm on the enclosed water.

Clustered around the pool were some cozy looking tables and chairs. Seated at one was Paul, who rose to greet me. He indicated that I should take the seat facing the sea.

"From that position the sunset should be perfect," he said.

As soon as I sat down, a young man appeared and asked if I would like anything to drink before dinner. After ordering, the man quickly - almost magically - disappeared. Paul took the seat adjacent so that we were facing the same direction.

"This is a lovely place," I remarked to Paul.

"Yes. Luckily they don't have guests here at the moment, so you can come over for a meal with their personal chef. This is a fantastic place to watch the sunset at certain times of the year. We might even get lucky and see a green flash today."

"I talked to others at my hotel about the mysterious green flash. Most thought it was a myth, as I did."

"No. It's no myth. I have spent many a night trying to convince people it does exist. It seems to me that we believe so much that is unreal these days and little that is proven. I'm never sure what people will believe anymore. We are in an age where you can reach out your fingers and find information quickly, and yet so much is believed without proof. We have become contradictory creatures, easily believing in unfounded pseudoscience and disbelieving ideas that a little research would show are true. We tend to accept only that which is familiar to us, with little critical thought."

"How do you decide what to believe then?"

"As I've said before, I'm a skeptic. If an idea can't be proven scientifically, I will consider the possibility of its existence but not become a believer. The scientific method and a skeptical open mind seem to be the only way to deal with the overwhelming amount of information available these days."

The waiter brought my drink, and I placed my hand around it, enjoying the cold feel of the icy glass on my hand. We lapsed into silence, both serenely watching the sun heading slowly towards the sea.

"So it's our last chat then before you leave tomorrow. What would you like to talk about?"

"I'd like to talk about you, Paul. Tell me something of your background. What were you doing before Roatan?"

"Ah. I wondered when we would get around to me again."

"Well, I've tried several times to talk to you about your past, but I can't seem get any details from you."

"Why do you want to know details about me?"

"People like to know who is giving them advice. How do you know these things? What personal story led you to take up handstands and live on an island? Frankly, they will be more curious the less you say; they may suspect that you're some kind of fraud or have something to hide."

Paul paused for a little while, then seemed to reach a decision and started to talk. "I was born in the 60s into a circus family. We traveled around, town to town, mainly through the lower states. At age 14, I ran away and went to school."

"You ran away *from* the circus?" I said disbelievingly.

"Yes. That's where I first learned about gymnastics. I worked a few jobs here and there to pay my way through college and ended up with a degree in psychology."

"So that's where you got your background training and interest in the mind?"

Paul nodded and continued, "But then a few things went wrong in my life and I ran afoul of the law. I ended up serving several years in jail."

"Did you change your name when you moved here?"

"Yes, and after arriving here, I became an underwater lumberjack."

"A what?" I must have misheard him.

"An underwater lumberjack. I had a thriving business here on Roatan cutting giant kelp and drying it. We sold it for nutritional purposes all over the world."

"That's fascinating." Leaning forward in my chair I asked, "How did you start doing that?"

"We started with a small team of guys bringing the kelp in by hand. It's very hard to gather, you know."

"Hold on," I interrupted. "Giant kelp doesn't grow on or around Roatan. It needs cooler water."

"Does it?" Paul said a small smile tugging at the corner of his mouth.

"You just made that all up," I said accusingly.

"Yep," said Paul now with a decidedly evil grin on his face.
"All of it?"

"Yep, all of it. And honestly, I cannot believe you were falling for it. Especially the circus bit. You must have already been thinking something along those lines to fall for it so easily."

"Why?" I asked. "Why were you making that up?"

Paul's mood turned a little more serious. "Yesterday, we were talking about cognitive biases. One of the well-known biases is that we adjust our conclusions on information we have been given depending on who supplies it. Sometimes this is useful. We learn to trust certain friends more than others, which is useful in our social interactions. We learn who are the gossips. Who can be relied upon to keep their word. Who speaks the truth and who lies."

"But how do we deal with information sources we are not familiar with socially? These days we rely on so much information from outside our own social circle and personal expertise. How do we assess the information given us? Marketers selling drugs know to put a wise or kind looking person in a white coat on the screen to convince us that a product is a good one. They don't even need to be real doctors. We may even suspect or know that they're actors, it doesn't matter. The bias still affects our decisions. This bias is often referred to as a *call to authority*. We are reassured when someone tells us something if they're in a respected position."

"If I told you that I had a doctorate in neuropsychology, you would believe my ideas were based on science and accept them readily. If I had studied in an ashram for years, you might think the same ideas more spiritual, and your acceptance would depend more on your own beliefs. You might be more skeptical of the ideas if I was a motivational speaker and you thought these ideas might earn me money. Each case may be true, and each case has no relation to the validity of what I have said. The messenger is not the message."

"All that may be true," I acknowledged, "but I want the details to round out my articles, not to validate what you've told me."

"Let the methods I have shown you stand on their own. Try them, research them if you like to ascertain their veracity, but above all, practice them. Only after attempting them for a period of time will you be able to judge their real worth. Let me remain a little bit of a mystery, that way I keep my privacy and you intrigue your readers."

The conversation was definitely not going the way I had hoped. Paul reached into his pocket and brought out what looked like a thin pack of playing cards.

"I brought these along, as I knew tonight was our last conversation, and I wanted to at least briefly cover some extra points. What I have told you is more than enough to make your life better, but I think it's necessary to keep growing. These are handouts for my last talk and have the rest of my foundations on them."

He handed the cards over to me. I pulled them out of a small rubber band that held them together and quickly looked through them. The top card had an illustration of a man doing a one-handed handstand on it. It was entitled: *Conscious growth*.

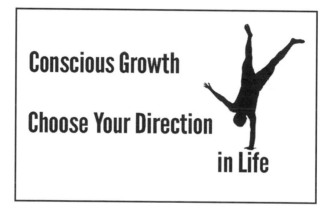

I glanced at the next three.

"Yes, I can see we have talked about the first four cards. Can we go through these others?" I asked.

"I thought you would want to. Pass them back, and I will summarize what I mean by them."

I looked through them and then handed him the next card. Double checking my small voice recorder was on, I asked him to proceed. He looked at the card I had given him. Twisting the card back and forth between his fingers, he began to talk.

Simplify your life

Wants are not needs

"Organize and simplify your life. People's lives are too complicated, our culture has gone to the extreme in consumption and personal choice. 'If something is good, then more must be better'. But it's simply not true. Too much choice paralyzes us and makes us dissatisfied with any choice we eventually make. Try to determine what in your life is truly important and simplify the rest, ridding yourself of wants that are not needs. One of the best parts about living on the island is that there is a lack of variety in items you can buy. It's one of the hardest changes for those who move here, but after a while, you realize you didn't need all of that *stuff*. If you simplify your life, it tends to make you focus on other things that are actually valuable.

He put down the card on the table in front of him "Do you mind me just talking at you like this? It makes me feel a bit like I'm being preachy or lecturing you. It seems strange when sitting at a table watching a sunset, but knowing you're recording it means I feel I can just keep talking."

"No, not at all. I can review it all on my recorder later," I held up the small device. "And this way I can concentrate more on what you're saying in case I have questions."

I handed him the next card.

Embrace difference

Live with contradiction

"Embrace differences. There are two points to this card. One is that I believe you should challenge your own beliefs constantly, and the best way to do that is to seek out others who think differently. It won't always be comfortable, nor will it necessarily change our opinions. We naturally and subconsciously filter our world, and tend to seek out that which agrees with and confirms our beliefs. To grow as a person, it is essential to strive against this tendancy."

"I think it's natural to hold desires and even beliefs that are in contradiction, because some of our own values can be contradictory. It's necessary to take a stand on some issues - just be sure you know why you do it. The reasons that others believe differently from you are usually because their values differ from yours.'

"Secondly, I try to live my life with these contradictory ideals. I believe that you need to enjoy every last second of every day, living each as if it's your last while conscientiously expressing gratitude for being alive. But you also need to plan your life as if you're going to be here for many years, and to act each day in such a way as to move incrementally towards those long term goals. These seem to be contradictory beliefs, but that's only because they're framed incorrectly. Living each day as if it's your last is not to discard all that we hold dear and live in excess and abandonment. It means embracing what we hold dear, leaving nothing unsaid and challenging ourselves as though we have only this one chance."

He reached for another card.

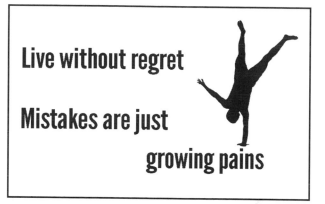

"Live without regret. Try new experiences. Put yourself into strange and uncomfortable situations. What's the point in being alive if you're not growing and learning? 'I wish I had tried harder to realize my personal dreams' is the number one regret of the dying. Don't let it be yours.'

"You will make mistakes. You are not living and growing if you don't have failures. Take courage from that fact. Change any failure into a learning experience, and you will grow. Don't fall into the trap of the 'I should've known better' *chant*. It's one of our cognitive biases that we believe in retrospect as if we knew all along what was going to happen. In reality, we do the best we can with the information we have at the time."

Health matters

Exercise each day,
    eat well and sleep

"If you're trying to change your life, the single best step you can take is adding exercise to your daily life. I don't mean some extreme workout. Even a daily walk would be sufficient. The physical and mental benefits of that alone would carry over into other parts of your life.'

"Eat right. I will not dictate how someone should eat, but there is enough research now for individuals to find food lifestyles that suit their needs. What you eat dictates your biochemistry and physiology to a large degree. So by considering carefully what you put in your mouth, you're adding energy and years to your life.'

"Lastly, do not cut back on valuable sleep. If you're sleep deprived, you do not process the day's memories and experiences correctly; you become impaired, and you won't notice it. . There's a reason the phrase 'sleep on it' exists. Yesterday's events are perceived differently the next day, and problems are often solved in the process. Or simply become irrelevant."

Be selfish

By serving others!

"Cherish your family and your loved ones. Create and join communities that support you emotionally. Finally, be selfish by serving others! It's a fact that acting generously and unselfishly makes people happy. Not just the one you're helping, but you. So if you want to be truly happy, choose to make giving a part of your life. Voluntarily helping others makes you happier, so I call it *being selfish to serve others*. If you don't have the time for big commitments, small acts of random kindness will lift your mood."

With the last card, Paul folded his arms. "There, that's it. I'm done! You have squeezed my mind dry."

The sun was almost touching the horizon. Sitting in silence, we watched the last five minutes as it slowly dipped down until finally, the last part of the sun fell below the edge of the water.

"No green flash again," I said.

"No, not today. Sadly, it was a perfect day for it. Only a few clouds in sight. But then, I've only seen a few in many years of watching."

"The sunset was beautiful," I reminded him.

Yes, it was. It's always wonderful just to sit and enjoy the sunset. I'm grateful I have been able to create a life that includes so many of them."

"Paul, one more question?"

"Sure what is it?"

"You asked about my beliefs and values earlier this week. But you didn't go into detail about your own. Can you tell me what it is you believe? Not the result of research or science, but what you believe."

Paul sat quietly for a while, eyes straight ahead. The color of the sky was changing from bright afternoon blue to a rich red. The few clouds were vivid yellow, lit by the hidden sun below the horizon.

"That's fair. You were kind enough to tell me your philosophy on life, so I'll tell you mine. I believe that our reality is an illusion. And please, I don't mean a metaphysical illusion."

He tapped his foot on the floor and his hand on the table. "I can stand on this solid floor, and this table is hard and tangible for you or me. If you hit your head on either, it'll surely hurt! But I don't believe that the thoughts in my mind can in any way affect anything physical and external to it. Though we all secretly wish we had super powers, just wishing for the universe to manifest something does not affect it in the least. If it did, fast cars, exciting jobs and beautiful houses would be popping up all over the place."

"By illusion, I mean that we create our interpretation of reality. If two people were to see an identical scene, they could create totally different experiences from it. I might be quite relaxed, enjoying the beautiful visual display of a setting sun, and you might be feeling sadness at your last evening on a tropical island. The physical reality is almost identical for both of us, but its internal effect on us can be totally different. In many ways, our internal construction is entirely separate and isolated from reality. We don't need anything to be happening in the external world to be experiencing tremendous feelings and changes within us."

Paul paused and tilted his head as if considering something thoughtfully. "I suppose an example of this is reading a book. Your eyes move over language printed on a page. Its physical interaction is limited to the feel of the book on your fingers, and some reflected light off the ink on the page. However, once those words are interpreted by you, the mind can experience a whole world of feelings and revelations. Where do they come from? Not the page or even the information contained in the writing on the page. Two people can read the same passage and have different reactions. Your mind creates those feelings and any revelations you feel are unique to you. So in essence, we create our own reality. This is hardly startling to most people. If you even think about how we experience the world, you realize it's all a fabrication in our heads."

"But we still share the same experiences, we just watched the same sunset," I commented.

"Merely the possibility of the same sunset. Our reality is still a fabrication of our mind. People seldom consciously think about how we experience the world. We subconsciously feel like we see out of two holes in our heads and listen through two other holes. We subconsciously feel there is a tiny person inside our skull peering out at the world. In fact, our eyes see light and turn it into chemical and electrical signals, and they move quickly through the brain. Where is the image we see? It's dark in there," he tapped his temple. "There's no screen inside the brain to project light onto, no hole to look through, no light at all. Just electrochemical signals in some dark organ surrounded by bone."

"Delightful image, Paul."

His face creased in amusement. "Our mind fabricates the image we see. We're like the movie *The Matrix,* except we are our own matrix. We create our own reality and that creation is sometimes wrong."

He paused again and called to the waiter to refill our drinks. I took the chance to interrupt him and direct his thoughts.

"You're telling me about how the brain works again. This isn't a philosophy, you're describing how we function not your belief system or your faith."

"Patience, my friend. I'm just setting the foundations. So, I believe that though there is a physical reality that exists, separate and unable to be influenced by our minds, I also believe that willingly or not, our brain creates its own interpretation of it. And specifically, an emotional interpretation of it. So my life is focused on choosing that interpretation, and manipulating that interpretation the way I want it to be. The way that I believe is more empowering and more enjoyable to me."

Picking up the drink that had mysteriously appeared while I was caught up in Paul's thoughts, I sipped, and I felt I knew where he was going from our prior conversations, but I wanted to hear the details from him. "So, how does this lead to your place in the universe, if you can you be specific?"

Paul looked round from where he had been staring while he talked.

"You are so not going to let me off the hook easily, are you?"

"No, I want to hear it all."

"Okay" he sighed. "First, as I have mentioned several times, I'm a skeptic. Knowing that the world I inhabit is an internal creation and can easily be flawed, I don't believe in much that is not provable and reproducible. My experiences are flawed. I know they are from all the research available. How can I be sure something is reality and not just my perception if it cannot be convincingly demonstrated on demand?"

"That's a very cynical way to look at the universe," I said before I could catch myself.

"Do you think so? Skepticism has been around as a discipline for a long time. Is it cynicism to know we are all flawed, and that to be sure of something it needs to be provable?"

"Let me give you a case in point. It used to be true that eyewitness testimony in court was the same as catching a person red handed. Even one good eye witness would be enough to put another person in jail for life. Why? Because it wasn't conceivable that a witness could be wrong, or lie when the stakes were so high. However, we now know that many people have been convicted erroneously on eyewitness testimony. We know that memory is not like a video recorder. We reconstruct our memories. Those memories are so easily influenced and changed over time by suggestion and circumstances, they're far from reliable, especially in such circumstances. So, if you can't reproduce something reliably and prove it to me, I reserve the right to doubt it."

"Secondly, I'm a semi-stoic."

I sounded that out questioningly. *"Semi-stoic?"* It sounded familiar.

"It's my own term. I'm a stoic but only half the time."

"Half of what time? I'm not following."

"The bad half. Or rather, when unpleasant things happen I act stoically. To me, being a stoic on these terms is that when unpleasant things happen, I accept them. I do not rage against them. I just accept and try to move forward. To struggle and fight something that cannot be changed is neither healthy nor empowering."

"We discussed this the other day, but I think it bears repeating. I find that people, myself included, are often paralyzed by our fears. Fears that are often unfounded, or never even eventuate. So if I find myself worried about some future event, I do two things; I evaluate how likely it is to happen, and if it's likely, I force myself to face in detail what I fear.'

"To control your fears, it helps to research and decide how likely this feared event is to happen. You may be being irrational, and once you know that, it helps. Some events are unlikely, such as a fear of shark attacks in waters that don't have sharks, or a general fear of a plane crashes To let fear in any way influence you and limit the enjoyment of life is just tragic to me.'

"Sometimes though, the possibility of a feared event is real. I could be worried about the consequences of a large action like a move, starting my own business, a change of career or any significant life change. In that case, I have a different strategy. I know we are terrible at predicting how we will feel in the future. That life is seldom as miserable as we think it will be, and that our minds can adjust to any new situation within a few months. With these thoughts in mind, I go through the worst possibilities of a decision, and what I would do if it came to those possibilities. By examining each possibility and thinking what my strategy would be, I'm able to handle my fears.'

"I use the term *semi-stoic* because a stoic presents the same front regardless of the situation. I refuse to do that. I will laugh with joy in a rainfall, let my heart beat thunderously in love, or swell with pride at the sight of my children. I accentuate the positive. I choose to be actively mindful of all the good things in my life. On a daily basis, I practice gratitude. I keep a mental gratitude journal. Every day when I wake up, I think of three things that I'm grateful for this morning. It can be as uncomplicated as waking up in a warm bed or as wonderful as having a family I love. Every night before I go to sleep, I think of three things that happened that I'm grateful for in that day. I try not to repeat myself if possible, but once you practice you will find that you know you're grateful for some particular people above all else. So it's hard not to repeat.'

"Do you know from our talks why I practice gratitude?" he asked.

"Yes, it's similar to the exercises you had me do at the start of the week. You are training your mind to look for and generate things to be grateful for in your life. You are directing your mind so that it's focused on them."

"Yes, like everything in life, the more you practice the easier it becomes. And after a while, you don't have to try so hard because you have trained your mind to help you out. I choose to see the bad things in life as something that will happen to everyone. I just try to accept them and move forward, but the good things I treat differently. I choose to enhance them and to amplify them."

"How can you amplify an emotion? Emotions are just a reaction to what is happening around you."

"First, by choosing to be mindful of the good events in my life and by paying attention to them, I'm telling my mind that this is what I want to focus on. Let me give you a simple and small example. You see a beautiful flower by the road. You could note its beauty and walk on, or you could stop and genuinely look at it. Be mindful of it. Understand what you find striking about it. Why it caught your attention. Then exaggerate your feelings for it. Feel them out and emphasize them."

"That's twice you have talked about exaggerating your feelings."

Pausing, Paul shook his head."Sorry, sometimes I jump ahead of myself, and I realize I didn't have time to teach it this week."

Paul shifted his body so he was looking directly at me. "Have you ever analyzed your feelings and how they're represented in your body?"

Puzzled still, I shook my head.

"Well, you understand that there is a close connection between your mind and your body. I find it amazing that there used to be a debate on this subject at all. But indeed, doctors used to deny it. Your body and mind are intimately connected, as the mind can alter your physiology and your physiology can alter the mind. They're in constant feedback. The mere act of throwing your arms wide and upright in the air like athletes do when they have won a race releases testosterone into your body and reduces the cortisol hormones. Such a small act can change your physiology."

"Have you ever wondered why emotions are described in physical terms? The excitement of *butterflies in your stomach, clenching your jaw in anger, trembling in fear*. All emotions have physical effects. In a real sense, the physical effects create emotions. If you hold a pencil between your teeth so that your mouth is forced into a smile and you sit across a table staring at a person for a period of time, it changes your initial reaction to them. Research shows that even though you have been forced to smile by biting on a pencil, you will actually leave that table with better feelings about them than if you had just stared at them. So next time you meet someone, smile! They'll like it, and you'll like them better.'

"You can learn to analyze the physical representations of your emotions when you experience them. Once you can understand how they're represented, you can even exaggerate the physical feeling, and it works like a feedback loop, strengthening the emotion. Practice enough and you can create emotions on demand."

"Create them? You mean you actually believe you can make yourself feel emotions out of nothing, with no stimulus?"

"Yes. Have you seen sports players psyche themselves up before an important game? Jumping up and down and shouting? Have you ever paced up and down talking to summon the courage to act? That's exactly what they and you were trying to do. Forcing ourselves into a different emotional state of mind is natural. But you can do it much more subtly if you study how you react when you have those emotions.'

"Next time you feel a little excited by something, try to identify the physical sensations that are your experience of the feelings. Where are they located in your body, what exactly does it feel like, try and find the words to explain them. Then actually try and exaggerate them. So if, you felt a little nervous fluttering in your stomach make it a little harder or faster. Play with the experience. If you stomach feels a little tight, then tense your muscles even harder. Play with each sensation until you think you notice a change in the actual feeling. As I said, with practice you can actually exaggerate your feelings or even create them from scratch."

"But that's artificially changing your emotions, it's not actually how you feel." I stopped mid-thought. Of course it was, that was his whole point. "Sorry. I wasn't thinking. It's all perception I guess."

"Yes, it's manipulation. The difference is that I'm the one choosing to do the manipulation. I want to make my life enjoyable and enjoyable for those around me. I want to make a difference in my life and others. So yes, I manipulate myself. If I don't, then fate will do it for me and I might not like the results. I have never enjoyed the phrase, 'happiness is a choice.' Mainly because people use it at inappropriate times. When something unfortunate happens to you, the last thing you want to hear is such a platitude. However, in a general sense, it's the truth. You can make a choice to have a happier future because happiness is a process or a frame of mind, not a final result. You may not be able to choose to be happy on any one particular day or even in one particular moment, but you can choose to be happier in your whole life."

With that, he eased back into his chair. I hadn't noticed him become so intense over the last few minutes. His philosophy was easy to understand. If we indeed create our own reality, then he was going to be the architect of that reality. He was not going to leave it to chance. He was going to make choices on how he would deal with the world. I knew many people who believed similar ideas, but I had never met anyone who had designed his whole life based around them.

Realizing that he was done talking, I thanked him for all the time he had spent with me over the week and promised him that I would try to practice what he had shown me.

"In reality, once you've started yourself down this path it's not that hard," he added. "As in most things, it's the getting started that is the hardest. You become better and better until most of the methods become second nature."

The sky, now dark, was full of stars. The lack of lights in the area revealed the sky in a manner that was entirely different from the way it looked back home, everywhere I looked, the sky was covered with silver dust.

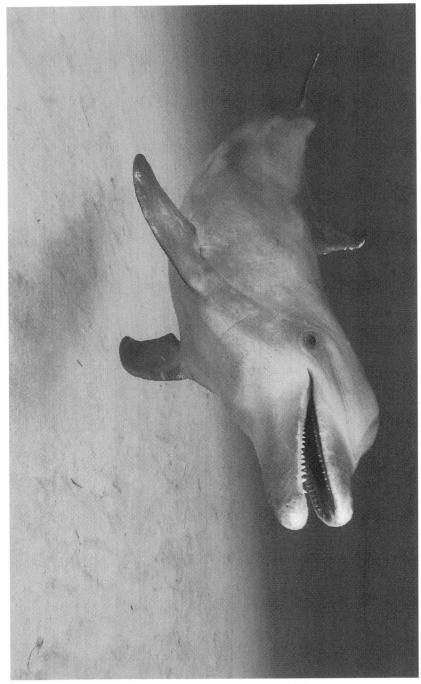

Swimming with the dolphins

10

The Final Handstand

It was almost 4 in the afternoon, and I would need to be at the airport soon to check in for my flight. My friendly taxi driver had picked me up from the Henry Morgan a little early and dropped me in front of the bright yellow Beach House in West End. Paul's call that morning had been puzzling, to say the least. 'I need a favor from you on your way to the airport. I will explain when you arrive. Just meet me on the dock.' It seemed fitting to end my trip on a mystery mission, and so I was happy to agree.

I ducked through the narrow passageway in the middle of the hotel and out the other side. Moving around the cafe tables, I stepped out onto the dock which merged into the back of the hotel. Left and right, Half Moon Bay swept out in its characteristic crescent shape. A wave of sadness hit me as I realized I wouldn't see this place for a while, if ever again. It was difficult to leave, and I understood all the fanciful tales I had heard of people who had come to the island, never to return home. I'd had a fabulous week diving, and Roatan had found its way under my skin. I knew my experiences in this place, and my conversations with Paul had changed me in some subtle way. A small seed of calmness and surety had been planted. I was going to use what Paul had shown me. I would probably get it wrong to begin with. It didn't matter; eventually I would get it right. Time was my greatest ally.

He was standing at the end of the dock with a large camera in one hand, talking to one of the local boat captains. He pointed to the camera he was holding, the sky and the boat tied to the dock. The captain nodded his head, then unhitched his boat and carefully walked it further down the dock away from the end towards the beach.

Paul saw me and waved me to the end of the dock. The sun was facing directly in front of me as I walked out and I realized I had dressed for the air conditioned cold of airports and planes. I was going to warm up quickly.

"Thank you so much for coming just before you leave. I'm not sure that I'm actually ready for this, but I feel you're the perfect person to help me."

He looked up at the sun, frowned a little. "Even if the timing is not quite right."

I gave him quizzical look.

He sighed. "Yes, I know I'm being cryptic. Just forgive me this last time?"

He handed the camera to me. "Do you know how to use one of these?"

For all its size, it looked like a standard digital SLR camera. "I think so. As long as it's on automatic, then I'm sure I can handle it."

"Good. You need to stand exactly here—" he pointed to a spot halfway along the dock. "I've set up the shot, but you may need to crouch down a bit since we are here a little earlier than I had planned. You'll need to be fast, as I'm not quite strong enough for this yet. I'm not sure how long I can hold it. But once you press the button, it will take shots quickly, so hopefully you will get one good one."

"Hold what exactly?" I asked

"Just point the camera and take the shot. When you see it, you'll understand."

"Okay," I said, not understanding.

Paul turned and walked towards the end of the dock. I moved to the position he had indicated I was to stand and looked through the camera.

""Wait!" I shouted "I'm facing the sun, it won't work. The pictures will be overexposed."

"No, don't worry. It has a special filter on, you can shoot directly into the sun."

I stood exactly where Paul had said, and, holding the camera to my eye again, I took a quick photo of his back. By the time I let my finger off the button, it had already taken three shots. It was extremely fast. Looking at the display, the image looked sharp, and the sun was in the shot. Paul was a covered in shadows, but I'm sure he knew that.

The end of the dock was a square shape, and he moved to a piling on the left corner where the boat had been. Standing in front of it, I could see from the way he was holding his body that he was breathing slowly in and out as he focused on the piling in front of him.

Slowly and deliberately, he leaned forward and placed his hands on either side of the piling, exactly as I had seen him do before on the Infinity dock. Then he quickly hopped up, pulling his knees up to his chest. Tucking his head between his elbows, he smoothly straightened his back and kicked his legs vertically into the air, forming a handstand. His body was perfectly in line with the piling.

I framed his body in the camera's viewfinder so that he and the end of the dock were in the shot. The sun was about two feet off to his left. Not knowing exactly what he was doing, I took another photo, which turned into four or five.

He was moving again, this time he gingerly lifted his left hand off the piling. His right leg was counterbalancing his left arm, and as he moved his hand to the left, his right leg moved a little away from his body. He looked a little shaky and paused for a second until he seemed to have himself under control, and then he gradually extended his left arm further away from his body at the same time balancing himself with his legs.

He pushed his hand further and further out until from my perspective, it was partially blocking the sun. Then it hit me like a bucket of cold water. I understood exactly what he was trying to do. He opened his left hand so that it was cupped, forming a half circle formed between his thumb and his fingers. I had to move a little to get the shot, but as soon as I was close, I pressed the button and kept my finger on the button. The digital camera make a rapid clicking sound as it took shot after shot.

Suddenly with a yelp, Paul lost control and fell backwards into the water. Rolling into a ball as he fell, he disappeared below the dock followed immediately by the sound of a loud splash.

I looked down at the screen on the back of the camera, desperately hoping I had been fast enough and got it right. I pressed the arrow button and flicked quickly back through the shots and there, before the last few shots of him falling, was the perfect shot.

On the screen, the tropical water and blue sky behind him, Paul could be seen clearly doing a one-handed handstand. His left hand, stretched out wide from his body, was holding between his fingers and thumb the sun.

I walked to the end of the deck, and Paul was just floating on his back in the water a little way from the deck and barely moving. His eyes looked up at me from the water.

"Did you get it?"

"It's perfect," I replied. "Just perfect!"

Paul shouted exuberantly and clapped his hand above his head, submerging himself in the process. He surfaced, spluttering and laughing. His joy was contagious, and I found a large grin on my face. He started swimming on his back to the dock. I watched him slowly drift backwards towards me.

What, I wondered, will he do? After finally achieving his goal after several years, what next? Then I mentally kicked myself. Really, had I learned nothing from him in our time together? I knew him better than that. It was never just about the goal. Sure, he would celebrate this victory, but it was just a part of the journey for him. His life was all about enjoying each day, and this was just a result of living those days the way he wanted to live them.

I put the camera down on the dock, held onto the piling with one hand and stretched the other one out to Paul below.

"Here Paul, take my hand!"

Paul grasped my wrist, and I held tight to his arm and pulled him up.

A Letter from the Author

I hope you enjoyed my book. A lot of time, energy, and pieces of my sanity were put into it. Quite unusually for an author, I actively encourage copying (piracy) and distribution through file-sharing sites. The paperback is available in hotel rooms, coffee shops, and other places for people to read without purchasing. I do this because I want people to read it. I can think of no better reward than knowing I have, in some small way, helped make a positive impact on a stranger's life.

If you enjoyed it but did not pay for it, ask yourself what you think it was worth: a coffee, a drink, a meal? I would appreciate it if you would donate that amount. Honor system - no judgment. If you are broke, I understand. Donate when you can. I have faith that there are better times ahead for you. If you have enough, earn some good karma by donating a bit more for those who cannot afford to pay.

But above all - share, share, share! Tell your family and friends, write a review on Amazon or GoodReads.com, email the e-book, torrent it, loan out or give away the paperback.

Please go to my website www.toholdthesun.com to donate or just to contribute your thoughts. Don't forget to say hi! I love to travel and maybe one day I will be couch-surfing in your area!

Warm regards,

Roatan 2013

Life on Roatan

If you are interested in visiting or living on Roatan.
Please contact Chas via email or Facebook.
https://www.facebook.com/ToHoldTheSun
www.lifeonroatan.com
Chas@lifeonroatan.com

New Book Releases 2014

The Master Fixer, the Red Berries and the Monsters

An allegorical novel on freedom and corruption.

&

Return to Roatan

We revisit Paul.

Check on Facebook for the latest updates.

read on...

The Master Fixer, the Red Berries and the Monsters

The President and the Vice President moved past the two statues that guarded the entrance to Academy grounds. The statues were four feet high, carved out of black marble in the shape of hands bent back at the wrist, palms flat and facing the sky. The symbol of the Academy. Soldiers escorted the men at a respectful distance on either side. Falling into step with the Advisor, the Cadet kept his voice low so as not to be heard by the President and the Vice President striding ahead of them.

"May I speak freely, Sir?"

The Advisor, dressed in his traditional flowing robes, glanced back at the young man who still had not left his teens. "I would strongly advise in the days to follow you speak freely and honestly at all times."

"I am not sure why I am here, Sir." His voice, though young, was self assured. "I heard what the Vice President said...", he caught himself, as if troubled by what he was about to say. "I can think of only one reason we would be here at the Academy, but that cannot be possible. Therefore..."

Cutting his words short, the Advisor interjected "I am sure your guess would be right. We are here to give the Master Fixer permission to leave the Academy grounds, something that has not been done in a hundred years." They walked on in silence for a while. The road curved back and forth. With each step the large black wall, which swept across the valley ahead of them, grew ever more solid and imposing. And with each step, the Cadet grew more and more restless. The Advisor, noticing his agitation, said, "Speak boy! There is not much time. I told you that you may speak freely with me!"

"I don't understand why I am here... and.. and why are they doing this, Sir?" This time his words were not so self assured, and he could not keep an edge of fear out of his voice as he spoke the last few words.

"Our leaders are doing it because they are scared. Because they can no longer hide that they are losing the war, because the monsters cannot be stopped, because we are losing control of our cities, because our people are being murdered and the fabric of our society is crumbling from the violence and fear that is spreading."

"Sir, the newscast says differently."

"The news lies."

"But why now? Why today? It's been almost 20 years since the war started, why now?"

The Advisor stopped, turned to face the Cadet and stared thoughtfully at the young man as if considering his options. Finally, he said, "Very few know but soon it will make no difference. We have kept it very quiet for reasons you will understand. The President's son was caught with berries, and tomorrow he will be one of those sentenced and marked so that all can see that he is a criminal and immoral." The last word held a hint of sarcasm in it.

The Cadet stared at the Advisor, now clearly horrified. "But his son is 18 like me, which means he will have to wear the mark of shame for life, and the President will have to resign his position as soon as it becomes known."

"Yes, the President is a desperate man. He is gambling his career by taking this action, hoping he can somehow save his son and stop the monsters in one stroke. In this matter, he is acting more like a father than a President, but whatever the reason, I think the decision is a good one. We are losing the war. It must be done." The Advisor, realizing they were falling behind started walking quickly to catch up with the others, who were by now having an animated argument as they walked. The Cadet quickly followed, and glancing back he saw that a large contingent of soldiers were following behind them. They moved with physical ease and discretion that marked them as the elite guard. The Cadet somehow found their presence comforting, easing his growing fear somewhat.

Slightly ahead on one side of the road was an area filled with large bushes. The bushes were covered with outcroppings of bright red berries. As the politicians walked ahead neared the bushes, they went silent; moving to the far side of the road as a group, they kept their eyes forward as they edged past.

The Advisor walked straight towards the bushes as the politicians walked away. The Cadet stopped and watched the Advisor in stunned fascination. Upon reaching the bushes, the Advisor did not hesitate as he strectched out and gently touched the berries with his finger tips. On the back of the Advisor's hand,a blue tattoo identical to the open hand symbol of the Acadamy could cleary be seen. The Advisor suddenly grabbed a handful of the berries and yanked them free. The Cadet caught his breath, paralyzed on the spot. Holding the berries in the palm of his right hand, the Advisor gingerly picked one up and held it up between his left thumb and forefinger, squeezing it until the juice burst from the berry,which stained his skin red. He licked his fingers, and smiled as the sweet taste hit his tongue, and his lips tingled.

"Advisor!"shouted the Cadet.

The Advisor turned to the distressed Cadet. "Compose yourself, Cadet.We are on Academy land. It has been many years since my student days here, and I have missed the taste of that berry."

The Cadet was aghast, "You could be marked for that. We could both be marked merely for being near that many bushes!"

The Advisor strode quickly to where the Cadet had stopped. In a stern voice, he said, "I was lead to believe that you were the brightest student of your year, that you had excelled in every branch of government, that great things were expected of you in service of the Republic after your graduation this year. Was I mislead? Did I choose unwisely?"

The Cadet struggled with his emotions, finally overcoming them and said in a defensive voice "No, Sir, you were not!"

"Where are we Cadet?"

"The grounds of the Academy, Sir, but..."

"Who rules here?" the Advisor said sternly.

Comprehension dawned on the Cadets face. "The Fixers, Sir."

"Good. You need to remember that at all times. The laws of

our democracy do not hold here. The Master Fixer has absolute power, and there is no law against touching and eating the berries here."

The Cadet, embarrassed, uncomfortably shifted his weight from foot to foot. "Yes, Sir, I understand. I apologize for my outburst." He swallowed and appeared to master himself, "I apologize I meant no disrespect. It is merely..."

"Merely that I was breaking our law." The Advisor said impatiently, "Yes I know, but you are too young to understand that when I was boy these bushes were found all over the Republic. My mother used to use them in her cooking. The taste is quite exquisite and brings a sense of vitality to the mouth that is hard to describe. Would you like to try one?"

"No, Sir!" said the Cadet horrified.

"Oh seriously, we are going to have to talk a little before we enter the Academy or you are not going to survive the next few days," said the Advisor in exasperation. "Come talk with me while we walk."

They moved past the bushes, the Cadet keeping a distance from them as he passed. Up ahead the others had not progressed that far, as their argument seemed to be slowing them down.

"The government of the Republic has only rarely invoked the Agreement," continued the Advisor, "and the last time was over 100 years ago. What do you know of the events surrounding the previous times that the Master Fixer was released?"

The Cadet seemed more comfortable showing off his knowledge and relaxed a little.

"I know that the intervention of the Academy and the Master Fixer resulted in lasting peace between the states and the establishment of the universal rights, " he paused and continued somberly, "and the last time it resulted in the execution of the President and imprisonment of half his cabinet."

"Hmm, I wondered how they were teaching that last event in the schools. What did your instructors say about why the Master Fixer executed him?"

"Very little. Our professors were not forthcoming on the

subject," he paused. "But they implied the Master Fixer had made a terrible mistake," he stopped as if he had said too much.

The Advisor laughed. "Yes. I can see that might be how some people viewed it, especially in schools filled with the children of politicians, but the Fixers do nothing without reason. The Agreement was created with a very serious purpose, and it is extremely dangerous. I believe the Fixers wanted to send a message to future Presidents. The President at the time and his cabinet enacted the Agreement in an attempt at personal gain, so the Master Fixer fixed the problem as he saw it: he executed the President. Capital punishment has been forbidden since the founding of the Republic, but the Master Fixer is above the law.

"But how could have done that - murdered him? Not only is it illegal, it is immoral!"

The Advisor stopped walking and grabbed the Cadet's arm, spinning him round, so he was looking directly into his eyes. "You need to be very clear on this, Cadet, once given permission, the Master Fixer can leave the Academy and do anything he wants; he can start a war, make or unmake our laws, imprison people, move whole populations at a whim. Whatever he wants to do, he can do, and when you keep that perspective in your mind, executing a politician for abusing the essence of the agreement was simply teaching a lesson in his mind."

The Cadet gulped, visibly shaken. "Yes, Sir, I understand."

The Advisor let go of the Cadet's arm and held his gaze for a few seconds. "I hope so. Do not fear unduly Cadet. The Fixers do nothing rash. It is not their nature. They need to understand the situation thoroughly first, but when they act, they will do so without hesitation, fear or favor. They seldom do what we expect or what we think they should do, which is why the Vice President fears this decision so much. He has been in charge of the war for years and has made no progress. The worst consequence of that execution is that it has made our current leaders too fearful of invoking the Agreement; it should have been done long ago."

After a pause, the Cadet spoke. "Sir, I do not understand why I am here."

Looking ahead, the Advisor saw that they were only a quarter mile from the gate. "Come. They are getting too far ahead of us. It is obvious that I need to explain your part in this, Cadet.

"Thank you, Sir. I was just summoned here today from university without any explanation."

The Advisor said simply, "I chose you and had you brought directly here. You are going to work as a liaison for the Master Fixer."

Dismay showed on the Cadet's face. "Why me, Sir? I am just about to graduate and have no practical experience. Surely, as an Advisor you would be far better suited to help him."

The Advisor held up the back of his hand displaying the blue tattoo on the back and replied, "No, as a failed student of the Academy, he would not want me. He will want someone who knows the workings of the current governmentand is young, hard working, open minded and flexible. Innocent even. Not someone who might be part of the problem."

Looking ahead at how close the gate was he said, "Cadet, you need to understand about who you will be dealing with. I do not have time to have a discussion with you before we get to the gate, so please let me sum up the important points with as little interruption as possible."

"Yes sir, of course."

The founders of the Republic believed that eventually any political system would face dire problems either from within or without. They knew they could not foresee all the problems that the future would bring, but they could foresee a way to solve them. They knew that one man with the interests of the Republic at heart, if given absolute power, could achieve much more than any group with differing desires. Yet no man could be trusted with such power, as eventually it would corrupt him.

So they sealed off this valley and created the Academy. It is a country within a country, with different laws and stands apart from the Republic. Its purpose is to forge a man that can be trusted for a time to wield absolute power and give it back.

"But Sir, I thought it was there to train the Advisors such as yourself."

"No," the Advisor laughed, "we are a byproduct of the training, the waste if you like. As senior students of the Academy, we are banned from ever entering politics, or amassing wealth, but we are respected and cared for as payment for our skills in problem solving and mediation."

"Only the children who show the most potential are allowed to try out for the Academy. The teaching schedule is so harsh that many do not manage the first few years, and drop out of the training, returning to normal life. That is no failure, as any student that has been in the Academy would excel elsewhere. The Academy is constantly testing and removing those that do not meet their high standards or who do not meet their emotional profile. At 16, the students are marked on the back of their hand with the open hand symbol as I was. The mark signifies that they are forbidden to enter into politics except in an Advisory role. For the next 5 years, each time a skill is mastered, a line is drawn on your hand and arm."

The Advisor showed his hand to the Cadet walking by his side. The Cadet leaned over and could see a few twisting lines emerging from the tattoo. He had not noticed them before because they had been hidden by the wrinkling and aging of the Advisor's skin.

"By the age of 21, a Fixer is an expert on practical human behavior. He understands the true motivations of people, behavioral economics, and group and crowd psychology. He studies the complex working of the functions of the brain. He is trained to be a master manipulator. The ultimate pragmatist, he is taught game theory to understand how to get the best result in any situation, and in the end, he is even taught the uses of terror and the horrors of war!

By the age of 30 a Fixer has completed training. Some stay in the Academy to study more and teach. Others are asked to serve the Republic as I have. Every 10 years, the most senior Fixers meet and appoint a new Master of the order, the one they deem the most skilled of them all. He will take up residency in the Academy and will be forbidden from leaving, helping the school and must simply wait. Wait for such a day as this.

"Why is he forbidden from leaving?"

"Has it been so long that they no longer teach the obvious in schools? What is the symbol every soldier wears on his uniform?

"It is the open hand, Sir, the symbol of..." the Cadet stopped mid sentence.

"Yes, Cadet. It's the symbol of the Academy. He is not allowed to leave unless expressly given permission by the sitting President simply because the Army is sworn first and foremost to the Master Fixer and secondly to the President and the republic.

The Advisor noticed the others were at the gate in the wall and said, "Hurry we need to catch up!"

The President had indeed reached the gate. The gate was twice the height of a grown man and three times as wide. A single thin seam ran down the middle. Both doors, dark and black, looked smooth and hard as stone. They were plain apart from in the center of each door, raised in gold, was an outline of a hand bent back and palm flat. The Vice President and the President were now in a full blown argument.

As they argued, the gate moved back as if sliding on ice and then swung inwards. It made no sound at all. The Vice President, seeing the gate open, grabbed the President's arm.

"You must not do this!"

The President turned, red faced, "Enough! You and your supporters have had as much money as you have asked; you have used the army, the police; we have created as many laws as you have needed, you have asked for more every year, and we have given it and more.For twenty years we have given you all you asked, yet now our children die or are corrupted, our cities darken and become unsafe; we are losing! The Monsters have crossed the borders and are beginning to control the cities. For every one, we kill, two take its place. We are losing!"

"But," the Vice President pleaded.

"I said enough!" shouted the President.

A man stood quietly in the opening where the gate had

been. He bowed gracefully. He was probably in his early 40's and was dressed very simply, in the same flowing robe of the Advisor. If he had heard the argument, he did not show it. He bowed to the President, smiled warmly and said, "We seldom have visitors. Welcome! How can the Academy help you?"

The President, recovering his composure bowed formally back. "We have come to meet with the Master Fixer, on a matter of urgency and importance. Please direct us to him. "

The man made no effort to move and looked around the group, his eyes taking in them all including the soldiers forming in ranks behind them. "Yes, Monsters sound like very urgent business. Indeed, I have never seen a Monster or known there were any in the Republic."

The Vice President moved forward abruptly. "Look Sir, just take us to the Master Fixer and stop wasting our time. This is important."

The man was totally unmoved by the outburst, as if immune to the other's emotion.

"I apologize. No deception was intended," spoke the man. "We noticed you arriving hours ago; your purpose seemed obvious, and I thought I would come down to the gates to welcome you personally. I had not expected to intrude on an argument. I am the Master Fixer."

He raised his right arm upright pulling back his sleeve as he did so. On the back of his hand was the symbol of the Acadamy, but from it swirled an intricate pattern of lines that trailed all down his arm.

The Vice President took a step back. The President said nothing, but he took out a folded set of papers from an inside pocket on his jacket and walked forward to the Master Fixer.

"Here is your permission to leave the Academy and the details of our problem."

The Cadet noticed out of the corner of his eye that the soldiers were moving to stand behind the President and Vice President, but his attention and eyes were locked on the Master Fixer.

The Master took it, opened it, and quickly scanned it. He looked back, appearing slightly puzzled, at the President..

"Monsters and Red Berries?" he asked, staring at the President. The President merely nodded.

"I have been asked, and I accept," said the Master Fixer formally and moved past the President and out of the Academy gates.

The soldiers behind the Cadet slammed their hands against their rifles and then thrust out their arms making the symbol of the Academy with their hands.

The Cadet felt sick with fear. In a single moment the greatest democracy the world had ever known, by the will of its elected leader, was for all intents and purposes under the power of an unknown dictator.

To be continued. Read on...

Return to Roatan

As I climbed out of the air-conditioned cab at the entrance to West End, the heat and humidity hit me like a blow. I knew it might take me days to become fully acclimatized to the weather. At least I had the sense to change from my travel clothes into a light pair of shorts, a t-shirt and the prerequisite sandals. I was going native already. The cafe where Paul and I had arranged to meet was a few minutes walk. Perfect. I wanted to take a short stroll and stir some memories.

There was a new road in West End; the rough sand street that had destroyed vehicles and ankles alike had been replaced with smooth concrete. Hugging the shore, it stretched in either direction from where I stood. If I turned right past the yellow beach house, I would be quickly at Sundowners, the bar on the beach where pretty much everyone ended at some point. Every place to meet was a bar, a restaurant or hotel on Roatan, I mused, which I supposed was normal for a beautiful spot on a Caribbean island. Turning left, I started down the road at a leisurely pace, the beach and sea stretched out to my right; the water was perfectly still and vibrantly blue.

The sun felt great on my face as I walked. I imagined the sunlight soaking through my skin and spreading out throughout my body, refreshing and healing as it went. I knew that was not happening, but Paul had taught me that reality was what you created, and my perception was often more important than the facts. I actually felt like stretching my arms out wide from my body and letting the sunlight trail from my fingertips as I walked. I laughed - maybe I take the visualizations too far sometimes. No need to look crazy to all the other tourists on the road. I felt wonderfully alive.

It had been too many years since I had been back on Roatan. Tomorrow I would start scuba diving. This visit I had the financial resources that I had lacked on my last trip. I planned to take some boat trips and maybe even head off island, but first I needed to meet Paul and see if he would help me.

Wooden buildings packed tightly together, filled with souvenir stalls, hotels , dive shops and bars cluttered both sides of the road. Some looked familiar, many were new. Paul had once told me that there was a high turnover of people here as they often thought opening and running a business on the beach was the ideal lifestyle. The reality was far different as they soon discovered.

"We are all here because we are not all there!" he had joked once. It had the sound of an old and worn phrase often retold to visitors.

I was not exactly sure where I was going, but Paul had mentioned it was a little past the Blue Marlin restaurant and bar. The Marlin was still locked up, as it was too early to be open. Later today it would be packed with locals and tourists alike, drinking, laughing and dancing, and probably some cringingly bad karaoke. The bars fed on the constant flow of new tourist blood to the island. The atmosphere changed weekly, sometimes daily.

I walked a little further along the street until I saw the sign for West End Divers on the left. Some wooden stairs wound up the right side of the dive shop. The Cafe Escondido, where we were meeting, was a new place to me but one of Paul's frequent haunts. Climbing the steps, I pushed aside a light curtain stenciled with a graphic of a giant Sumo wrestler and was instantly hit by a welcome blast of cooling air from a huge fan rotating on a stand in the corner. It slowly covered the room in a lazy back and forward motion. An espresso machine hissed loudly. The air was full of the aroma of coffee and tantalizing cooking that made my mouth water. The cafe was located on a large balcony looking out over the Caribbean. In addition to the six tables, there was a couch and hammock for the patrons which gave the cafe a relaxed cozy feel.

Paul was sitting with his back to me at a table that overlooked the water and the road below. One hand rested on a book that lay on the table. He seemed lost in thought, staring out over the docks and water taxis towards the horizon. I quietly weaved around the tables until I stood directly behind him.

"Anything else you need, sir?" trying my best to imitate a server.

"No thank you, I am fine." His head turned slowly from the water view as he answered me, a small smile playing on his lips. "But you are welcome to join me."

I sighed. So much for my fooling him. Rising to his feet, he grabbed my outstretched hand firmly and pulled me into a big hug.

"Great to see you again. It has been far too long." He motioned to the road. "I saw you walk up. One of the reasons I enjoy this place is that I can watch the people from here without being seen. I find it fascinating.

"That's borderline creepy, Paul!"

He laughed. "I guess it would be if I knew the people, and I was spying on them, but I don't. I will probably never see them again apart for these few minutes, a small window into their life. Yet in that tiny moment, I wonder who they are and what their lives are like.

I pulled out the chair on the other side of the table, sat down and took a few seconds to really look at him. It had been a few years since we had met, and if anything, he looked better.

"You look good. How is life on the island?" I asked.

"Not many major changes here, that's why I like it."

We ordered a round of coffee, passed on the offered food and spent some time catching up on each other's lives. Paul had taken up yoga and was finding it rewarding but difficult, which I found amusing for a man who could do handstands. I brought him up-to-date on how my writing was going and my life in general. After a while, we had covered all the obvious points, and there was a lull in the conversation.

"I am happy to see you again on Roatan, but I have a feeling this is more than a social visit. What's up?" asked Paul.

I sat back in my chair and fiddled with the cup in front of me.

"I am not sure what exactly I want, Paul. Last time I was here, I learned a way of living that has helped me grow and enjoy my life. But there is something..."

Paul waited patiently for me to finish my thought.

"It is hard to put into words, but you helped me understand

myself, and I wondered if you could help me understand others."

"Others?"

"Yes, other people. My work often requires me to interview people and write an interesting and fair view of them, but to be honest sometimes they drive me crazy. Their belief systems are incomprehensible to me. I can't get inside their heads. They seem to be irrational, and honestly I often think there is something wrong with them. But then I think maybe it is me, maybe my thinking is too rigid, maybe I am the one that is crazy.

I stopped talking, feeling that I was beginning to ramble a little.

Paul just sat still, staring at me. I was beginning to feel uncomfortable and more than a little foolish.

"Can you help me?"

"Yes, I think so," he paused considering. "We can talk about how to be more understanding of other peoples' perspectives and maybe more flexible in your thinking. I believe I can even help you comprehend peoples' motivations, but there are two things you need to accept. First, you can never know another individual's thoughts. All I can help with is a general understanding of others that may or may not help you in your quest.

He stopped. I nodded my understanding. "And the second?"

He smiled. "You might be right, you might be crazy."

Acknowledgements

I wrote this book as a gift for my children, who are ungratefully leaving my home now. Publishing it was an afterthought. I am not a writer. Well, unless you call a child presenting his mother a charming but disfigured clay figure a sculptor. His heart may be in the right place, but he lacks the skills. So the publication depended on the skills of others. Lots of people have contributed to it directly and indirectly, far too many to mention in detail, and I am sorry if I omit you in some way.

To Toria Sweeny for coming out of nowhere to save the day and the world from my defiling of the English language.
My test readers, who pulled no punches and sometimes I even listened to: Ms. Kelly, Jeremy, Laura, Melissa, Jenny, and Dan!
Annick for being my friend the grammar nazi and taking time to make many, many corrections after it was published.
Jordan for sitting with me through the corrections and offering helpful suggestions. Father son time!
Shawn, for the use of his amazing photos of Roatan
My children, whose mere existence has saved my sanity more times than I care to remember.
Ms. Kelly who held my hand through some of the darkest times in my life until I emerged the other side.
My brother and sister-in-law, Kip and Helen, who just always seem to be there when needed.
Al and Jeannine, for just being great.
My Mum, Nana B, Andy and Paola for being my loved family.
Mini and Tim for being uniquely Mini and Tim.
Susan, for being there when needed, no questions asked.
Nicky, for being the model for the cover handstand.
Joselyn "Joss" for some wonderful times.
John and Barbara, for being the best friends you could ask for.
Terry, for being my drinking buddy and escape from reality.
Edison for helping me with the island language.
Laura cheerleader, listener and a role model for my daughters.

Gaby, for the gift of joy and her 3 year old smile.

The people at Coconut Divers for helping Kaela. PJ, Gay, Marco, Rags, Sigita, Tree, Ted, Keith, Will

...and of course Vernon and the Book of Dude, for being an inspiration.

Lastly, just general life thanks and gratitude to my friends and those that helped my family and in no particular order:

Phil B, Myra and Tom, Tricia and Ceasar, Guy, Phil, Andrew, Patty, Kat, Jessica, Jeremy and Melissa, Bob, and Sonia, Vilma , Mike B, Nancy, Kendall and Mark, Will and Loren, Tim, Kate, Lloyd, Celeste and Milosh, Chris, Scotty C., Zac, Aaron and Christine, Ms Daine, Josie, Lezli, Liz, Keila, Marianne, Laura G., Adina, Marc, Mark, Ron and Bonnie, Merari, Carol L., Carol K., Brett and Verity, Ely, Piero, Sivia, Karl, Brad and Tiff, Maura, Tony, Mathew, Wendy and Tommy, Zak, Louis, and so many more...

The JavaVine coffee crew Alex V, Quentin and Wyonna, Anita, Merlin, Pasquale, Kirby, Murray, Jay, Dan

And my friendly bar staff (yes I am sucking up) Tiger Tim, Ezra, Eddison, Derry, Sandra, Sheba, Zebby, Tracy, Virna, Christine, Adam, Kristen "Fred", Ed, Tita, Rick, Vincent, Stephen.

About the Author

Chas Watkins was born and raised in England and is a naturalized Australian. His children are all American, which he finds very confusing. He moved to Roatan nine years ago. He has an unused degree in electronics from Hull University in England and has somehow managed to work for many fine and good companies without being fired. After the raging madness of the dotcom world of California, he moved to Roatan to settle with his family. Chas currently pretends to work as a realtor and radio DJ. He reads an awful lot, watches the sunrise every day, likes a beer with friends and drinks too much coffee. He runs on the beach in the mornings, practices handstands, and lives happily on Roatan with his cat Gary and the children that have not yet deserted him. Even on his best day he is nothing like Paul, but strives to be so. If you are really unlucky you may meet him, and whatever you do, don't offer him a drink as he is a very rude and uninteresting person.

24422987R20094

Made in the USA
Charleston, SC
25 November 2013